# THE
# FIRE-TRIED
# GOLDEN
# HEARTBEATS OF
# GOLDEN AGERS
## AT THE SUNSET OF LIFE

## REV. BENJAMIN A. VIMA

 www.trafford.com
North America & international
toll-free: 1 888 232 4444 (USA & Canada)
fax: 812 355 4082

# CONTENTS

To my dearest benefactors and friends who have become God's favorites as they have reached the golden age and are full of years. In particular, I remember with gratitude and love all the golden-agers at Montereau, Tulsa, to whom I am granted by God a golden opportunity to perform the caregiving ministry as one of their chaplains. I too warmly recognize the awesome, chivalrous services done in love and dedication toward the physical and emotional welfare of golden-agers by the staff and employees of Montereau.

# FOREWORD

## Background of the book

Serving almost fifty years as God's laborer in His vineyard, I have been discipled by Jesus, my Master, to work with Him in many capacities as pastor, preacher, writer, musician, and performing artist. Very specially, He has offered me a unique task of being caregiver, counselor, and healer to golden-agers full of tears in many parishes around the world. The most striking call from my Master, through my superior in the church, has come to me recently—to go, live, and serve the golden-agers as their chaplain in the prestigious center Montereau, Tulsa. I have accepted His call willingly, and at present, I am humbly, proudly, gratefully, and joyfully performing my caregiving tasks among my friends full of years.

## The title's singularity

On this splendid backdrop, I began writing my fourteenth book, which contained the deep thoughts of people over seventy, like me, as we ran the race even at our sunset moment. I sought out a title suitable to the book's contents. In the early years of my youth, almost every person over fifty was identified as old. Indeed, it manifested rudely the fact of their getting closer to the grave. At the end of the nineteenth century, that kind of horrible views died down because, as a result of the Enlightenment and because of scientific and medical discoveries, "getting old" started at sixty-five. Later in the twenty-first century, people were found living robust, active, and energetic lives as in their youth days even after seventy.

Hence, according to a current research, old age started at seventy-four. In the meantime, modern society—based on the morals "give respect and get respect"—started searching for the right term to classify or categorize the modern young-old people in the globe. It made sure that the choice should spell out most correctly the identity of people over seventy and more, and it also should be the best term that is nonoffensive, proper, appropriate, respectful, and politically correct.

In my deep study of finding such a term, I came across so many terms in colloquial usages and in official records, such as "elders," "older adults," "seniors," and so on. After many hours of browsing hundreds of articles in the Internet, regrettably, I ended up in more confusion because there were many debates about and pros and cons for every term. In those critical moments, I found the term "golden-agers," which seemed to me much closer to all the conditions for my choice. This was the story of the title *Golden-Agers*.

## Fire-refined golden heartbeats

In world history, we read so many heroes and celebrities who have written their memoirs, which are full of their thoughts and deeds. And so are the biblical heroes who have poured out so many of their holdings about God and their failures and successes in abiding by God's premonitions and promises. At the brink of death, they cry out for the strong and saving presence of God; at the same instance, their hearts rise with grateful beats for God's positive promises for them. I can honestly say that I myself, as one already entering the threshold of golden age, hear the same heartbeats from my inner spirit as well as from so many of my peers. This book contains one hundred of such *fire-tried golden heartbeats*. They have been gathered for more than ten years and intensively worked on as I begin my retirement. They are framed as small articles under many titles.

## Presenting the book as a love gift

Overenthusiastically, I have packaged the articles with TLC as a book for my friends—young and old—as a gift of love. I offer it to the young ones so that they can either fight against them or bite with them or munch or even digest them to get stronger in their Christian faith. Here, I remind my young friends of the appreciative words of Pope Gregory the Great about St. Benedict: "There was a man of venerable life, Benedict by name and grace, who from the time of his very childhood carried the heart of an old man." It is absolutely correct to say all of us get more wisdom in our golden age to live honorably. However, to start it in youth is the greatest blessing from God.

As for my colleagues, the golden-agers, I present it to them so that these heartbeats of mine may join their own, making their inner holdings wrap around and get stronger or dance according to the beats as a sort of spiritual exercise in their lone world stage.

Also, since this work addresses directly the golden-agers, especially their dreams, issues, holdings, values, and difficulties—their golden age—I believe this book will be of great help to all the beloved caregivers who minister to their golden-aged spouses, siblings, parents, and friends.

My only request is just take each article a day from this book. Close your eyes, sleep with it, and rise while singing with gusto, "Alleluia! Praise the Lord!"

Your friend, being refined by God's fire as you,

Rev. Benjamin A. Vima

# SECTION I

# ABOUT MY GOD AND HIS

# 1. God Is a Mystery of Mysteries

I believe there is God.

He is not some kind of force, wisdom, energy;

He is one but in three persons.

I can talk to Him, and He can also talk to me.

Don't ask me how. I can say it is a mystery.

He is the beginning of the whole universe,

But He has no beginning.

He is the Creator of everything, every creature,

But He is not created.

He commands me to obey His willed statutes,

But He wants me to act on my free will.

He knows everything of me,

And He has predestined everything for His purpose,

But He cannot keep me away from doing evil.

It is again another mystery.

I am OK with these multiple mysteries of God

Not only because I believe

In scriptures and traditions

But also because I am content considering,

While I myself and my life are mysteries,

Why not add some more to them?

# 2. A Global God

A critic of God

Can never be a genuine and legitimate one;

He is worth nothing

If he has not learned or at least been informed of

The nature, quality, and behavior of god figures

As professed in all religions and religious sects.

The critic behaves as a blind man;

Touching one organ of the elephant,

He judges its total shape and quality.

Hence, being God's apologist and servant,

I strongly hold

God is not a single property of a single religion;

His identity is spread around

In every bit of historical efforts

Taken to expound God.

He is all, He is everything, He is beyond the gender.

He is all in all; He is a global God.

He is beyond the universe, beyond the space;

He is beyond every religion's theology and practice.

God is all in one and one in all.

God is a common good; God is the majority.

God is life; God is total power.

God is love of all loves;

God is all over again.

# 3. My Idea of God

I choose the idea of God

And put my whole life in it

Because of my dreams and cravings

To know everything about all things and

To possess them totally and holistically.

Stunningly,

There are billions of issues

About me, about others, and

About the entire creation.

Very unluckily,

Because of my limitations and weaknesses,

I cannot realize those dreams instantly and fully.

The factual truth is

Every intelligent person is capable of taking

Only one tiny part of those above-listed issues;

One dissects it, analyzes it, conquers it,

And finally possesses it

As one's own knowledgeable property.

Even when that person's product reaches me,

I hear it, read it, sometimes analyze it, and digest it;

Then I try to possess it.

Funny thing is

That also becomes a tiny, little part of the whole.

Hence, being a smarty,

I try to bundle the billions of issues;

I name it "God"

And try to possess Him as much as I can.

# 4. Wrong Views about God

For so many years in my religious life,

I have been brainwashed by some believers' group

With some childish holdings about God:

First, God is a genie working instant miracles;

He hides Himself in a very large space lamp

And delivers some of my wishes here and there.

In every religion, there are many small miraculous lamps

Like sacramentals, sacred places, and holy things

In which their big genie stays

And offers as many wishes as the devotees crave for.

Second, God is a Santa Claus.

This is an easygoing belief system

That does not endorse

Any intimate relationship with God.

"If I am good, I get lots of gifts from Santa."

Thank goodness,

When I have become consciously matured,

I have always blamed myself

For believing God as somebody He is not.

Then I have realized

When I hold such wrong ideas about Him,

I have to face two problems about living faith:

One, I feel despondent at times

When Genie and Santa don't respond;

Two, I am filled with remorse

For making God look like an idiot.

This is why I am very careful

Not to join those groups of perverted faith.

# 5. The Estate of the Lord

The Lord's estate is

A workplace of fortune,

A treasure island,

A Garden of Eden where

All creatures move and have their being,

A grove of trees

Being planted near streams of water,

Bearing fruits in season and out of season.

Whoever labors in it does prosper.

What is my position related to this estate?

I am only a coolie

Standing idly around on the roadside,

Waiting for my chance to be hired

And recruited by the Estate Owner

At His discretion and in His proper time.

# 6. The Hilltop House of the Lord

What is the house of the Lord?

It is a house of morality, a house of dignity,

A house of love, a house of joy.

Who is fit to dwell in that house?

It is none other than

A person who practices virtue

And speaks honestly,

A person who spurns what is gained by oppression.

Persons residing in God's house

Brush their hands free of contact with a bribe.

They are the people who close their ears,

Lest they hear of bloodshed.

They are also those who close their eyes,

Lest they look on evil.

It is God's truth:

This house of God is built on the mountaintop.

Its height is immense and as tall as the Lord.

He has also asserted humans can ascend;

Plus, He has shared with us the highway route

To get to His hilltop house.

We share our bread with the hungry,

Offer home to the oppressed and the homeless,

Clothe the naked when we see them,

Never go the way of sinners,

Never follow the counsel of the wicked,

And never sit in company with scoffers,

Trying to be clean of hand and pure of heart

And desiring not what is vain.

I feel God expects too much from me,

But His Son stands by me and says,

"Come to me, and bring your burdens to me.

I will make your 'mountaineering' easy."

# 7. The Magical Morsel of God's Word

I am too careful to deal with the Word of God

Because I know well it is a "two-edged sword."

Besides its marvelous positive effects,

It also will bounce back at me

With unthinkable negative results

If it is not properly listened to and complied with.

While some of the Bible versions

Preserve the Hebrew word meaning "morsel,"

Other versions translate it as

"Little food," "fragment of bread," "piece of bread."

Whatever the differences in translation,

It is very interesting to notice

How fittingly it brings out the glory of the Word.

In the book of Genesis (18:5),

We hear Abraham telling guests,

"Now that you have come to your servant,

Let me bring you a little food,

So that you may refresh yourselves;

And afterward you may go on your way.

In the book of Judges (19:5),

We hear from a father-in-law,

"Fortify yourself with this little food."

And in Proverbs, we read (17:1),

"Better is a dry morsel, and quietness therewith."

But we read in John's Gospel (13:27),

"After Judas took the morsel, Satan entered him"

To plan the betrayal of Jesus.

From the above-mentioned scriptural verses,

Taken in a metaphorical way, I understand

The morsel of God's Word, received with pure heart,

Becomes a means of refreshing and fortifying;

Otherwise, it brings out pernicious effects

If taken in with a contaminated mind-set.

# 8. The Faith Jesus Taught Me

Jesus defined and proclaimed His faith

As chutzpah; that means

A crazy relationship with another person.

In this kind of faith matter,

I humbly but shiveringly follow my Master.

It surely is not cool in the beginning,

Yet it demands from me a persistent faith in action.

There is one craziest thing about chutzpah:

It demands an "obstinate fidelity" in my loving God.

It is like the mind of a lover expecting his friend

To be continuously with him.

To avoid it, Master warns me,

"Don't make some lame excuses

As a playboy does to his girl, saying,

'I love you

If the color of lips that I prefer is there,

If such and such charming aroma is around there,

If the moon is still bright in the sky,

If the meeting site is cozy and unpolluted,

If I am OK on that particular day and time,

If everything is OK around the world.'"

And most importantly, I am advised

Not to put any condition for loving God, who prefers

Unconditional lovers as Jesus has been.

Hence, if I have decided to love God with chutzpah,

I must abide by His single condition:

"Love me with your whole heart, whole mind,

Whole soul, and whole strength."

This sort of mind-set should be

The base and core of chutzpah.

And Jesus wishes me to uphold it

To survive in God's amazing love.

I have almost surrendered to my Master's wish.

# 9. The Story of My Dealing with God

Here is a brief confession about my life with God:

I, as a child, was seeing God

Only in my parents, priests, nuns, bishops, popes,

Preachers, elders, and peer group.

Though late, in my middle age, I liberated myself

From all conventional controls over me

And behaved as if I was a free human being.

The result was

I began slowly drifting away from religion,

I saw God in a fog,

I denied God's existence,

I ignored God's presence.

A time arrived

When I started rethinking my life's survival,

And so I decided to hold on to God as a survival kit.

A little later,

I found God walking with me.

I was sure I cannot live without His nearness,

And so now

I make attempts to possess Him as my Life Partner;

This means, surely,

I crave for frequent intimate experience with Him.

As for my future?

I leave it in my Partner's hand.

# 10. Jesus: Who Is He to Me?

In Jesus, I discover

All my human dreams come true—

About God, about His mercy,

About His concern over humanity,

About His promises,

About His permanent presence

In the midst of humans,

About His sharing by incarnation.

For instance,

I am confined to Jesus because

He is truth in flesh,

He is eternal life in spirit,

He is the truthful and spiritual way toward that life.

Moreover, God's truth is abiding in Jesus;

He has proved it is possible in me too.

God's way to reach my human destiny

Has been revealed in and through Jesus.

God's life, to be lived and

To be enjoyed, is in Jesus.

He is the container of God's quality life.

He has proved God's life can indwell

In ordinary human flesh.
He has been a pattern
And medium for me
To encounter a godly life in my life's chores;
Therefore, I never stop crying out to Him,
"Amen, amen!"

# 11. The Love Beyond

My absolute faith is my God is "all-beyond";

Therefore, I name Him "God the Beyond."

As scriptures call Him "love,"

His love also must be all-beyond;

Never do I prefer, therefore,

His love to be constrained to

Onetime traditional explication and

To religious practices—past, present, and future—

As the Father's love is

Beyond anything and everything,

So the love of Christ surpasses

All knowledge (Eph. 3:18–19):

It is beyond the universe

And all historical experiences of it.

It is beyond Sunday or Sabbath Day.

It is beyond any love I chase out among humans.

It is certainly beyond my imagination.

It is beyond any of my

Human communication and arts.

In sum, it is beyond

Any human, cultural, and historical experiences.

I am well aware of my puniness

In knowing about God's love, so I confess

I cannot understand the mystery of it

With my own ability; however, I uphold

I should be true to my tiny, little knowledge of it.

I still continue my pursuit of

Going deeper in that knowledge.

Plus, with Paul, I am convinced that

God will grant me strength to comprehend

The breadth, the length,

The height, and the depth of

God's love in Christ.

# 12. The Long Rope

God offers me a long rope.

He does not compel me or let me feel burdened

By His coercion or by His "terrible" presence.

He walks with me, He laughs with me,

And indeed, He weeps with me.

He even stands there when I commit sin,

Not even smacking, hitting, or spanking,

Though He has said (Prov. 29:15),

"The rod and reproof give wisdom."

As the prodigal Father, He has kept silent;

But later, I have come to know

His merciful silence is not eternal.

However, at my freelance sinning times,

I am fully aware

He laughs within Himself at how stupid I am,

And He pities, saying,

"This little rascal doesn't know

What exactly he gets into."

God holds enduring patience and mercy with me.

He continues to provide His blessings

As the sun bestows light to both good and bad men.

Even at the times of my drifting away,

He lets me go as far as I can slip away.

Until I return with my free will,

He stands at the door waiting for me.

When I regret and feel sorry for all my blunders

And pledge to be His housemaid,

He extends His loving hands to me.

In hindsight, I recollect His deal:

He has bestowed me a long rope of mercy with which

Either I can climb up from the sinful pit as Peter

Or I may commit suicide as Judas.

# 13. Being Shy Is God's Trait

I don't mean God is bashful or timid

As a junior high school boy at a party.

God has been seen publicly speaking

In thunder and lightning. But fortunately,

When He shows up to me in person;

He is shy to intervene in my privacy.

God's rest, we hear in Genesis,

Is not to be esteemed as

The chronological end of His creation activities;

Rather, it is the goal of creation:

rest of peace and harmony. And so is

His silence, slowness, and stillness in my life.

Very rarely does He encounter me

By intervening directly;

Mostly, He speaks and acts unquestionably

Through His favored messengers.

Surprisingly, many times in His deal with me,

He uses people who are not in His camp.

His direct intervention comes astonishingly

Only after cries, lamentations, and prayers of many

For days, years, decades, and even centuries.

I know now why: He recognizes well

My limitations and acts according to them.

He is invisible, spiritual; but I am physical, material—

Such a vast difference between both of us, yet

He descends to be with me, lowering Himself to my status.

This is like my relationship with my cat:

I can talk about Cat, but I cannot talk with her;

Cat also cannot comprehend

What it means to be human.

The all-powerful God finds the same difficulty with me.

How is it? Ha ha ha!

# 14. The Litany of God and Mine

"I am who am, in you, with you and for you."

This has been a surreal mantra of God

Very close to my heart.

I continuously hear His voice within my spirit:

"My New Age man, I go on loving you,

Providing you, and caring you always.

Whether your mood is out or in,

Whether you are good or bad,

Whether you obey me or not,

Whether you understand me or not,

Whether you make right or wrong decisions,

Whether you know the why of my silence or not,

I am always there for you, in you, and with you.

What else can I say?

I know you dislike me

In your times of troubles, problems, and failures,

For you don't understand my behavior and motives;

But you should be convinced that

Even when you dislike me and run away from me,

Still, I am there with you, in you, and for you."

At those rumbling words of God,

My humble and feeble heart beats rapidly.

"Almighty God, I am bewildered

And find no words in response.

I can recite only one single mantra in trembling:

'Thank You, Lord. Thank You so much.

Here I am for you to do Your will.'"

# 15. How Good It Is!

This is the day the Lord has made.

*It is good; it is good.*

This is the earth the Lord created.

*It is good; it is good.*

This is the life the Lord has breathed.

*It is good; it is good.*

This is the moment the Lord has blessed.

*It is good; it is good.*

This is the body the Lord has prepared for me.

*It is good; it is good.*

This is the home the Lord has placed me in.

*It is good; it is good.*

This is the family the Lord has knitted me to.

*It is good; it is good.*

This is the love the Lord has shown me.

*It is good; it is good.*

This is solely because,

At the end of His every creative action,

Our Creator shouted out,

"It is good! It is good!"

# 16. Every Creation Is Sacred

I profess

The whole humanity and the whole universe

Is part of the Whole—God.

In every bit of the creatures

Made of atoms and neutrons,

Filled with minute particles of being,

However tiny the living creatures,

Their complex organs—constituting

Blood, bones, veins, ventricles, and so on—

Have been touched and blessed by God, the holy.

Hence, I shouldn't deny their sacredness

Unless they break free from their Creator.

This is why I am thoroughly convinced that

I have to do something

For those "creaturely particles" in the universe,

Especially the humans who

Try to grow in the stature of God

As their ultimate end

And fullness of "particles."

This kind of belief forces me

To sacrifice and part with

My time, my talents,

My treasures, my entire life even.

That is the only way as my Master has dreamed

I can be fully sacred as God is.

# SECTION II

# ABOUT ME AND MINE

# 17. My Religious Journey to Its Peak

In my youth, as a cradle Christian,

Following some elders of my religion,

I performed all religious practices

As a fledgling chick with

Underdeveloped wings of fear,

Maybe with some duty consciousness,

Or by a certain pressure of social obligation.

But after I matured in Jesus's discipleship,

I understood that true religion is

Gratitude-filled consciousness of

God's active presence in me

And among my fellow humans,

His loving interactions, and

His powerful proactions performed

And still being performed under the sky.

Getting closer to my golden age,

I am thoroughly convinced with James (1:27):

"A religion, that is pure and undefiled

Before God the Father, is this:

To care for orphans and widows in their affliction; and to keep oneself unstained by the world."
Though it is late awareness,
It is still not too late
To live and end my life
In such a beautiful and pure religion.

# 18. The Absolutes I Strongly Uphold

There is fullness of life only in God,

Yet my innate human nature indeed

Longs for possessing that amazing life.

This unbelievable dream is

Not at all a fake or unreal one.

It arises purely from my exquisite faith that holds

I have been created in God's image and likeness.

This is why, even it is bitter to my brain

My heart beats for it rap-style

And sings it with sweet, angelic melody.

It searches for it everywhere—

Up and down, north and south, east and west.

Very interestingly, this admirable and precious

Fullness realm of the Supreme is

Encircling and pervading His entire creation.

To my mind-blowing surprise,

As I absolutely and in awe believe,

The legitimate key to

Such sublime and unfathomable realm subsists

More within me than anywhere.

But as a hidden treasure, it is buried in my soul.

# 19. Consecration of My Life's Jiffies

I take every moment of my life,

Especially

The time of troubles, crises, and trials,

And offer it to God as Jesus has done,

Esteeming it,

First,

As a source of redemption, namely,

I share in the sufferings and death of Jesus

For the redemption of others and myself,

And, two,

as a source of sanctification;

That means

To make my life's

Particular moments and movements

As a living sacrifice of

Glory and praise to the Father

For the purification of

My interior self, consequently

Transforming my earthly strides into

A source of self-satisfaction and contentment

And, above all, taking each step of life

Toward reaching my "hilltop."

# 20. My Belief Is Full but Not yet the Fullest

I believe in God, who lives in me—

Not only in me but also in my neighbors.

Not just living,

He also exists all in all, all through all, and all as all.

If so, logically, as even church fathers have claimed,

I want to say daringly

I am in a way a god or godly person. To utter this,

My brain trembles; my tongue is tightened.

I understand the reason of such feeling within me.

It is nothing but the consideration of God's

Unfathomable wholeness, His immense allness,

His immeasurable goodness, and His superb holiness.

In other words,

God can never be contained,

And He can never be matched.

I and other human beings made of clay are

Only a tiny little part of Him, the Whole.

Never can I claim I am He,

Nor can I allege I know everything about Him.

Rather, I am only in His likeness; and
Certainly, I am in the process of becoming godly.
Such enlightened belief leads me to profess
I contain God within me as an eternal seed
And cooperate with His Spirit in its blossoming
Until hopefully, one day, I will contain God fully.

# 21. Revisiting My Religiosity

From the nineteenth century, intellectuals and pundits

Claim the religious system as

A violation of human rights,

Exploitation of ignorant people,

Deception of innocent/naive people,

A basin of lies,

The cause of horrible hatred and division,

A distraction from or distortion of real spirituality,

An institution of slavery,

A carnival of predators.

Nonetheless, I feel—

Though the above-mentioned claims

Are a little far fetched and prejudicial—

There is a certain truth about them.

I myself have been encountering,

In my religious circle, flaws:

They are superstitious,

They are hypocritical,

They are only otherworldly,

They are vagarious (wishy-washy).

But I am strongly convinced that

These criticisms and reproaches against religion

Can be fully erased and brushed out of sight,

Especially in my personal religious milieu,

If I, in the light of Jesus's Gospel, regularly

Revisit my religion,

Reread it, rewrite it,

Renew it, and relive it.

# 22. Being with God

Undebatably, I possess a "being" from God

Temporarily hidden but eternally active.

It is surprisingly a conspicuous absence;

I recognize I am what am. This is because

I am made in His likeness and image,

He is forever and has holistic fullness;

I breathe and survive through His Spirit, and

With Him, I move and have my being.

Most mind-bogglingly, in my prayer time,

I consciously get to be near God;

Despite His physical absence,

I feel His living spiritual presence.

Maybe it is a sort of mystical encounter;

Certainly, it is not a mistaken elucidation either.

I know fully well that

Just as a scintilla can't claim to be the whole,

So too I am unable to demand.

In no way I can avow that

I am "being God," the totality of being.

Nevertheless, I firmly believe

I have been endowed by God with an awesome ability

By which, if I strenuously strive *being in God*

As His favorite portion and inheritance

And if I faithfully obey His command of love,

Loving my neighbors as myself,

A miracle will occur one day.

I may be summoned by the Whole

To be absorbed into His absoluteness

As all other humans who are part of the Whole

Who do the same.

We, His parts, have come from Him,

And so we will join the Whole.

# 23. The Memoir of Human Crosses and Resurrections

Human history is simply a package of

Crosses and resurrections,

Big bangs and bit bangs—

Cross and resurrection of civilizations,

Cross and resurrection of kingdoms and politics,

Cross and resurrection of sufferings and wars,

Cross and resurrection of human frailties,

Cross and resurrection of families,

Cross and resurrection of neighborhoods,

Cross and resurrection of beauty,

Cross and resurrection of arts,

Cross and resurrection of unanswered prayers,

Cross and resurrection of popularity,

Cross and resurrection of poverty/emptiness,

Cross and resurrection of unfulfilled dreams,

Cross and resurrection of convictions,

Cross and resurrection of parenthood,

Cross of deaths and burials—

But ultimately ending with

Resurrection to eternal life.

# 24. Faith and Trust Are Synonyms of Victory

I have been gifted with friendship of

So many fellow Christians

Holding staunch faith in religious traditions;

However, regrettably,

I have noticed the core of their faith

Gradually fading,

Treaded underfoot.

In the midst of the challenges

And needs of earthly life,

They begin living a whimsical life

That is neither hot nor cold;

They are irresolute and unsure of

What they hold as life's values.

Certainly, I don't want to be included in that crowd;

Hence, repeatedly, I read the Bible

And make scriptural words my heartbeats

Because they are the secret of success in life:

"Unless your faith is firm,

You shall not be firm" (Isa. 7:9b).

"Trust in the Lord, your God

And you will be found firm.

Trust in his prophets

And you will succeed" (2 Chron. 20:20b).

# 25. An Inactive Person Is a Walking Dead

Some people chronically oversleep

As Rip Van Winkle, who has slept through a revolution;

People in the past have just been sleeping.

Sages have told about them:

It is possible for humans to go through life

As if in a coma, ignorant of the depth of life;

Many abhor them like prisoners walking

As they are taken to the death chamber.

Scriptures ascertain the same

But in a different context. Paul says (Eph. 2:1),

"You were dead in your transgressions and sins."

He means all of us can be spiritually dead

While physically alive. We may be moving around

And doing the chores lively;

We can still be interiorly dead because of sins.

But God expects us to walk alive, even if we are dead,

Turning into dead bones to life (Ezra 37:10–12).

He can bring us back to life as He has sworn.

Very sadly, the postmodern age is full of dead ones.

Am I among them? Quite frankly, yes, I am.

Am I ready to rise and walk? Sincerely, yes, I do.

But the problem is I cannot do it by myself.

I hear the call of the Life Giver to Lazarus:

"Wake up, shake off dull sloth. Look out,

While the sun shines on you."

He disturbs my cozy sleep.

He doesn't let me stay put as a couch potato.

I have no other way to go.

I have to be awake, rise, and walk.

The reason—He is my loving Master.

# 26. Wild Dreams Fulfilled

A woman was asked by her friend,

"What kind of man do you want your partner to be?"

She replied,

"To others, he must be a lion.

To me, he should be a squirrel."

This is the kind of raider wish I dream of.

I desire others to be easily

Packed, bundled, and parceled to fit into my pocket;

I long even to crush the entire universe

Into a fruit juice maker and drink it

Whenever I feel hungry.

I romanticize squeezing

All beauty queens of the world into one princess,

And I should own her as my exclusive lover.

In the same way, many times, my brain fantasizes

About God, the Supreme Being.

Stunningly, the scriptures say

My wish has already been granted.

About my dream of the invisible God

Coming near me as one like me?

Scripture says to me,

"Word became flesh and

Made his dwelling among us" (John 1:14),

Plus,

"Behold, the virgin shall . . . bear a son,

And they shall name him Emmanuel,"

Which means "God is with us" (Matt. 1:23).

Besides,

I dream I should get a portion of His Spirit.

Scripture assures, "I will pour out

A portion of my spirit upon all flesh" (Acts 2:17)

Thus, my wild dreams seem to be answered.

# 27. Pragmatic Reasons for My Charities

Reason One:

I try to earn and save earthly treasure

In and with Jesus because I know

"Whoever doesn't gather with him scatters."

Reason Two:

God bestows me

More blessings—spiritual and material—

So that, in turn, I can play the role of His proxy

In sharing His blessings with the needy.

I am sure when I give, I am given; He promised,

"Give and gifts will be given to you;

A good measure, packed together, shaken down, and overflowing, and will be poured into your lap."

Reason Three:

I will be now remunerated for my generosity;

That is what my Master has promised:

"Amen, I say to you, everyone who has given up house . . . for my sake . . . will receive

A hundred times more now in this present age."

Ultimate Reason Four:

I consistently hear the words

Jesus has declared to Zacchaeus, who has promised

To share half of his possessions to the poor:

"Today salvation has come to this house."

# 28. Give Break to Deeds Not to Break Yourself

As most of my friends,

I am a busy bee.

C. S. Lewis has well said some decades ago,

"If the devil cannot make us bad,

He will settle for making us busy."

Thinking I am honest to Jesus's call to awake,

I am not only too awake

But also too busy.

Because of modern information explosion,

I am stuffed with and drowned in information

To fill my brain with knowledge

About everything and anything in the universe.

I take fake pride in

Being on the top of all issues,

News and views under the sky.

The result?

There is a chronic tension

Stealing away the rest and peace from my heart.

Plus, regrettably,

The same busyness that makes me tensed

Does not permit me to deal with that tension

In preventing or curing it.

Every moment God shouts out to me,

"Settle down.

Be still."

And my Master's continuous invitation is

"Come with me and rest awhile."

Let me give myself a break—indeed, a holy break.

# 29. Investing in Heavenly Willow Street

I confess sincerely

Often, in my past, sometimes even now,

I have been mostly investing

My time, my money, and my talents

To covet earthly and temporal rewards—

Such as

Self-gratification,

My bodily pleasure and entertainment,

My enslavement of humans and pets—

To solely satisfy my unsaturated hunger

For honor, glory, popularity, supremacy, and so on.

Like so many humans, I seem to be focused on

Building an abundance of

Earthly treasures and pleasures.

But in the light of Jesus, I am aware

No true Christian can live that way.

I am ready to bank now with Heaven because

Jesus, who runs the largest investment firm,

Which is customer friendly and trustworthy, exhorts me,

"Sell your belongings and give alms.

Provide money bags for yourselves

That do not wear out.

An inexhaustible treasure in heaven

That no thief can reach nor moth destroy."

# 30. My Practical Spirituality

It's nothing but the Catholic Christian spirituality.

It consists of three major phases of actions:

First, I should approach God with

"A sincere heart and in absolute trust,

My heart sprinkled clean from an evil conscience

And my body washed in pure water."

Second, I should hold unwaveringly

To my confession of faith

That gives me hope,

With strong conviction

That He who has made the promise is trustworthy.

Third, I must

Love my neighbor with no discrimination,

Exactly not only as what Jesus has exhorted

But mainly as how He has loved me.

Very importantly,

Not absenting myself from my assembly,

Which consists of my micro- and macrofamilies,

I should rouse us

To love and encourage for good works.

# 31. Human Absolutism

I hear very often in media, when questioned,

The interviewees answering with the adverb "absolutely."

The human fact is

Everyone wants to assert one's own opinion

As if it is an absolute truth he/she holds.

Surely, this absolutism is

An important factor in my human dealings.

Nothing in my life that is productive or surviving

Can be without absolutism;

For example,

Unless I feel absolute about what I sell,

It won't be bought.

Unless I am absolutely confident

That my undertaking will finally succeed,

I will not accomplish it.

Unless I consider absolute what I believe in,

I will not get its benefits.

However, I also must keep in mind

This factor of absolutism can be a destructive one

As any other tool in my hands.

It should be generated from love and honesty.

Plus, it should proceed with the same two.

If not,

It will become a source of destructive results

Such as terrorism, wars, and infighting.

Hence, I am very cautious in handling

Even my religious absolutes.

# 32. My Noteworthy Ability before God

I can very easily "adulterate"

God's plans, His choices, His courses and works.

But I can in no way "alter" them.

I can pollute them but cannot change them.

What is designed by God will happen.

I do not have any hand in it.

In this perspective,

I know I will die; I cannot do anything about it.

Perhaps I can quicken its arrival;

I can even liquidate its painful moments.

Above all,

I can achieve unthinkable victories at its brink,

Like Cathlin Hakkins, a resident of Florida.

She was diagnosed with brain tumor.

Doctors fixed a date for her demise.

Not minding such deplorable life condition,

She decided to win a degree before her death.

That was her final ideal to be fulfilled.

She studied hard. She got the degree one day.

A few days later,
She died in peace and contentment.
I don't know how far the brink of my end is,
But I resolve I will continue to do the best,
The most I can, till the Lord arrives.

# 33. My Natural Belief System

When I say I believe, I mean
To hold on to certain things beyond
What my senses behold now
And what I hold now intellectually and religiously.
I cannot be without believing.
I may say I don't believe in
God, religion, scriptures, any story, or any values.
However, I can never escape from believing them.
I cannot but believe them because
My survival in this world largely, why, even totally,
Depends on believing and trusting;
Therefore, I must start believing
Strongly, boldly on what I just now believe in.
It may be in money, politics, relationship,
Popularity, glory, philanthropic efforts,
Creating, inventing, publishing,
Innovative arts, crafts, and sciences.
And certainly,
I too can believe and trust in
The totality of all
Those above-mentioned categories,
Which I love to call God.

# 34. A Dream That Woke Me Up

In one dream, I saw myself imprisoned in a dark cell,

Imagining, comparing, contrasting my status

With others who live in wonderful light.

Suddenly, I looked up; I noticed

A tiny, little sunlight through a small window.

I was fixed to it, felt comfortable;

And I was satisfied with it.

I didn't even try to turn to the darkened backside;

I died there looking up to the window. I was buried.

I saw in the same dream another man

Being put up in that uncomfortable small, tiny cell;

He was not satisfied with the window light.

He looked to the darkness anxiously,

Moved left and right, scrambled around the cell.

There it was.

At one edge, he found a door completely opened.

He was freed; he left the cell to the fuller light.

I woke up. I saw myself still lying in bed.

Then and there, I decided

I should never give up my search for a fuller life

Because I know my life here is

Only a process and not a product.

# 35. What Is My True Happiness?

If my recollection was sincere and truthful,

For the many past decades,

I esteemed my happiness consisting in

Getting positive post mails or e-mails today,

Chatting with lovely and understanding persons,

Receiving calls from friendly people,

Collecting a fat check or cash as surprise gifts,

And stockpiling appreciative words from others.

A day came with a shining light

To ask myself,

*Is that all my life?*

"Not at all," my inner spirit answered.

After a few times kneeling,

After many times strolling in solitude,

I came to the realization that

I should eagerly long for

An in-depth knowledge of life itself.

The main reason is,

More than all that I do and get for my happiness,

To enjoy my existence of every moment is

The rarest gift of the Creator.

# 36. Keeping My Religion Alive

Before trying to keep something alive,
I should find out whether that something
Is already dead or dying.
When I start adhering intently into my religion,
I should dig into its status in today's milieu.
In this, I shouldn't act as a photographer
But as a lab scanner; I must see through it
Not with imagination or creativeness but in reality.
This work of scanning must be performed
Not just through my religion's common language
And not by the scale of certain traditions
But with the mind-set of today's religionists—
Their worldview, their Gospel-value-based deeds,
And their reason-based thinking.
They will perhaps offer more impetus
To practice the living faith of my religion.
I firmly uphold this way of judging my faith
Only in the light of Christ, who has uttered,
"People will come from the east and the west
And from the north and the south
And will recline at table

In the kingdom of God" (Luke 13:29).

He challenges with His sovereignty

All who highly esteem their faith (Luke 19:39–40):

"If the crowd keep silent, the stones will cry out!"

In other words, Jesus states very clear to me,

"Your faith is good, but to get better, humbly

Let others' simple faith clean up your untidy faith."

# 37. Committed Discipleship

As any disciples committed to Master Jesus,

I hold an attitude, vision, and mission

That are centered on this:

All from Jesus,

All for Jesus,

All in Jesus,

All toward Jesus,

All by Jesus,

All through Jesus,

All with Jesus,

All is Jesus.

Because of such belief,

I visualize spiritually that

Jesus is in all,

Jesus is for all,

Jesus loves all,

Jesus has died for all,

Jesus gives to all,

Jesus lives for all.

Because of that kind of visualization,

I see Jesus in others,

I hear Jesus in the cry of the poor,

I obey Jesus in good and truthful leaders,

I hug Jesus in success and failure,

I unite with Jesus in death and life,

I foresee Jesus coming in my final hour.

# 38. Why Do I Follow Jesus?

Through His amazing incarnation,

Jesus has renewed the face of the earth:

Through the Virgin Mother,

He has brought forth a new birth

Through His miracles,

A new power

Through His suffering,

A new patience

In His resurrection,

A new hope

In His ascension,

A new majesty

Subsequently.

Not only has He renewed the human culture

But He also has become the culture itself

And granted me, by God's grace,

To become a cultured person.

In short,

He has become my culture, an embodiment of

My attitudes,

My actions,

My habits,

My traditions,

My etiquettes,

My manners,

My arts,

And everything that makes me great.

Are they not sufficient reasons to follow Jesus?

# 39. Am I a Sheep or a Goat?

On Judgment Day,

Jesus will separate us one from another

And place us as the sheep on His right

And the goats on His left.

I ask myself, "What am I? A sheep or a goat?"

Sometimes I cheat myself, saying in my soliloquy,

"Maybe the physical Benji is a goat

But not the spiritual Ben."

I think that is totally wrong.

I am both physical and spiritual intertwined,

Which can never be separated from each other.

As long as I am living here on the earth,

I am a blend of both "goatness" and "sheepness."

However, from time to time, there is a possibility for me

To jump out of my "goatfold" to the sheepfold.

How is it possible?

Jesus's Spirit has already given a clue for it:

"Charity covers multitude of sins" (1 Pet. 4:9).

Hence, this is what I do:

Love and care for the needy and, if need be,

Sacrifice all possessions,

Including myself, for their welfare.

I may be a goat under the veil of charity,

But factually,

I turn out to be an unblemished sheep

Being washed by Jesus's blood

Under the shadow of the cross.

# 40. My Kind of Faith in God

There are different kinds of faith in its velocity:

Little faith, light faith, solid faith,

Serious faith, valid faith, and so on.

What then is my faith?

One thing I know

About the reality of faith as scriptures propose is

It demands from me a total surrender.

If this fact is not recognized and cherished by me,

I become victimized,

Lonely, weak, useless, good for nothing.

With this troubling backdrop,

I uphold a faith that is

Simply an awareness of God's presence within me;

It is a consciousness of His love around me.

Enhancing its quality, I lift it with perseverance;

It starts from me and ends in me.

Since I put my whole heart into my faith in God,

I take my conviction very seriously.

I work on it; I don't fluctuate about it.

I don't doubt it either.

Surely, I don't disturb it in any way.

I live in it, I chew it, I grab it, I dig in it.

But never have I dug out from it.

This is my "genuinely certified" faith.

# 41. Connection between Life and Sacraments

According to my scriptures and traditions,

God has been communicating with humans

Through patriarchs like Abraham and Moses,

Through prophets and kings,

And finally through His beloved Son, Jesus Christ.

The content of His communication has been

Nothing but grace.

If I join spiritually His life, death, and resurrection,

I will be saved by His amazing grace.

Certainly, by Christ's church, which is

An ensemble of rituals, devotions, and practices,

I receive God's benevolent grace.

This is why the church is proud of calling herself

As Christ's sacrament.

In all my participation in sacramental practices,

I get God's answers to my quest,

And I give my response to His covenantal love call.

The effects of sacraments can be realized fully

By my wholehearted participation in them,

Above of all by transforming my daily chores

As a living sacrifice of praise and glory to God.

# 42. My Tabor Experience

Let me testify
The Tabor experience of feeling good is
Not physical but mystical.
As Peter has begged Jesus
For such "feeling good" permanently,
Many times in my prayer time,
I too feel it's so good to be here.
In the ecstasy, Peter has been talking about others
And not his own security or safety.
In the same way, I forget and
Lose myself completely at that moment
As what life partners feel in their orgasmic moments.
Many times, I enter into the darkness as Abraham, who
Has felt terrifying deep darkness enveloping him.
When I get sight of the risen Lord,
I lose my own sensual powers
As Paul has lost his eyesight.
Before the Tabor experience,
I will have been an enemy of the cross;
But after it, I befriend
The sufferings and warmly embrace my crosses.

After such transcendent encounters,

I feel being left alone;

And because of some strange behavior,

I am considered by others crazy, freak, and so on.

Tabor experiences never let me

Use natural tactics of politics

To win over others

And become number one.

At the end of this astronomical happenstance,

I hear loudly the order of Jesus:

"Don't tell anyone."

That puts my big mouth shut.

Thereafter, I start living happily, contently

Mainly because I resolve myself never to be

The focal point in my life's undertakings.

# 43. Divided but Can Be Healed

I am one

But divided as body and soul.

My family is one

But divided as different personalities.

My nation is one

But divided by languages, races, castes, creeds.

Humanity is one

But divided as haves and have-nots.

These divides, we think, can be solved

And healed by some genuine solutions.

However, those solutions have proved

Aborted in the historical efforts such as

Religious slogans,

Secular humanistic philosophies,

Communism, and so on.

Here are the real solutions,

I feel, to heal the divides:

I believe that divisions can never be solved;

Hence, I should learn to live with it,

And I learn to love as well as hate it.

I don't pretend to be

An incredible unifier or pacifier.

I don't cheat others with

All kinds of empty promises as solutions;

I follow the norm proposed by Pope John XXIII:

"Omnia videre, multa dissimulare,

Et pauca corrigere." He meant,

"I am fully conscious of all divisions.

I close my eyes toward many of them,

But I try to do something."

Sure, I will integrate certain divides

That hurt me and others,

Especially those divides

Existing within me and outside of me

For which I too am responsible.

That is all I do, and I will do it till I die.

# 44. Surrender in Dealings with God

My Master instructs me through His life

To surrender to God as my life's priority;

He too asks me to include in this surrender

My failures, my failings

My disappointments, my unresolved hopes,

God's seemingly eternal silence to my cry,

And my own wait for His touch.

This is my challenge in the race of spirituality.

However, my Master doesn't preach to me

To surrender life's challenges and to stop there;

Rather, I hear Him say

To continue my pursuit of fullness and happiness.

If down the hill I slide, I should try

And try again and again to climb up the hill;

I shouldn't lose heart and give up at any point.

At His admonition,

I don't shake off my hope;

I won't lose sight of my destiny, my dream, my goal.

I just go on abiding in God's close connection

By constant practices that may be

Most of the time,

Mere sacramental, just virtual, and far fetched.

However, my Master's hush-hush message is

"My friend, don't feel downcast.

Our relationship is in good shape.

You and I are getting closer and closer, integrated

As vine and branches."

# 45. Awesome Contest in Door Knocking

Jesus exhorts me (Matt. 7:7),

"Knock and the door will be opened to you."

The same Jesus's Spirit says (Rev. 3:20),

"Behold, I stand at the door and knock.

If anyone hears my voice and opens the door,

I will enter his house and dine with him."

The question is, who wins first, God or me?

I have found out the apt answer to this:

There is a picture hanging on my bedroom wall;

Its title is "The Invitation."

In that picture, inside a luminous hall

Banquet is going on with sumptuous food.

At its entrance sits a crippled person

Whose hand is being lifted by Jesus, who

Invites him to come in and participate in the banquet.

A scriptural passage at the bottom of the picture reads

"Blessed are those who have been called

To the wedding feast" (Rev. 19:9).

What I understand is "door knocking" is

A win-win situation between me and God.

While His disciples knock at God's door,

God too knocks at the doors of their hearts.

This is an eternal game God and I play;

Often I play it as child's hide-and-seek game,

But God faithfully knocks at my heart's door.

When both simultaneously open our doors,

Astoundingly, we encounter each other in intimacy.

# 46. Godly Authority

In childhood, I was strangled by authority phobia.

While some of it still stays,

Most of it has been cleared out.

During this slow process of healing,

By my continuous analysis,

I became aware of four phases of my life growth:

First, there was a period of dependence,

In which I felt feeble and incapacitated, so

I depended on others for anything and everything.

Inevitably, I worshipped others as God's icons.

Second came a period of independence

In which I became full of myself and preferred

To proclaim, standing up on the rooftop,

"I am authority to myself.

I make and shape my own destiny."

It was very short. But then came the third phase;

I labeled it as a period of "on-dependence."

I started experimenting with my authority over others.

I made them feel dependent on me;

I felt great in this foolhardy perception.

Fourth came a period of interdependence;

I started interrelating with others,
Giving respect, and getting respect mutually.
I realized humans share equally a godly authority.
While I demand obedience from others,
I too have to submit in obedience to them
For reasonable and right causes.

# 47. Freedom to Live Fully

"Lazarus, come out," Jesus said.

Immediately, the dead man came out

But with tied hand and foot with burial bands,

And his face was wrapped in a cloth.

And so Jesus said, "Untie him and let him go."

Let me put myself in the place of Lazarus.

He was alive but wrapped in binding cloths.

He needed help getting free of them.

By baptism, I have come out of the death tomb;

But still, I am bound

By certain unwanted attitudes and behaviors.

I have to find them and rip them off.

I recognize some with which I am tied—

Pleasure-seeking tendency at any cost,

Self-centeredness and self-pity,

Insensitiveness to others' needs,

Concentration on my self-glory and popularity,

A quitting syndrome when life challenges me.

Thanks be to God. In my "untying efforts,"

He has sent me many disciples of Jesus to assist me.

Like me, there are so many friends

Still tied and unable to be freed fully.

They are eligible Lazaruses to get assistance,

To be untied to breathe freely,

And to walk and even run in the life race.

Jesus is constantly calling

You and me to assist them.

# 48. Why I Am Prone to Reject God

While God has been eternally longing

To hold intimate relationship with humans,

Why do humans, as I, reject His intimacy?

In my deep analysis, I have discovered a valid reason:

Besides time calculation and physical space,

There exists a vast gap in the spiritual realm

Between God and me.

Even though God descends to the humans

To perform love deeds among and with them

And to relate intimately with human souls,

He has to be what He should be:

He is "I Am who Am." He has to preserve His

All-holiness, all-highness, and all-powerfulness.

He cannot contradict Himself. That is His justice.

The Bible points out whenever He comes to humanity,

The earth trembles; nature stutters.

That way, His ways and paths are straightened out.

"Who will endure the day of his coming?

For he is like the refiner's fire . . .

Refining them like gold or like silver" (Mal. 3:2).

Whenever human attitudes and traditions

Are straightened out for His onboard trip,

There will occur in individuals and societies

Certain tremor, confusion, tension, and even fear.

It is a kind of discomfort, insecurity

That cannot be tolerated by any human.

Perhaps this may be the reason

Why I have been rejecting God's intimacy.

# 49. Loving Sacrifice-Based Singlehood

The first truth about singlehood is
All humans are individuals and social animals;
This means in no way that the so-called singles
Never withdraw from their social identity.
I am one among millions of singles under the sky.
Becoming single happens in many ways.
Singlehood is chosen deliberately
By many like me for higher causes;
Many others turn out to be single
Because of natural causes such as
Birth defect, divorce, death, and social injustice.
Regrettably, so many problems arise for singles
When they misconstrue their status.
Take me for example; when I was first instructed
To take the vow of celibate singlehood
As a prerequisite for serving as a Catholic priest,
I felt that kind of initiation was totally wrong.
After becoming fully aware of its ultimate goal,
I felt happy to be so
Because it is nothing but a pursuit of
Experiencing God's love totally.

Also, it is a continuous and strenuous pursuit of
Fulfilling God's will.
In that process, my singlehood becomes
A status of wholistic commitment to Jesus.
I embrace my single status
As a loving, living sacrifice to God,
The same thought I share with
Many of my single friends. I also tell them
In whatever manner they have embraced such
Magnificent rank of intimate friendship with Jesus,
In this, they must hold the same attitude as Jesus's own.

# 50. My Terrible Misgivings and Misdeeds of the Past

In my younger days, I loved

To act as protagonist in stage dramas;

But unfortunately, the play directors found out

I was good at performing as the antagonist (villain).

In fact, audiences cheered me for my cruel, viperous acting.

I mentioned this past of my life because

I was in reality, in my daily engagements

With my peers and relatives,

Very timid and mild in behaving and conversing.

A time came when I got awareness of myself

Having been exploited by others.

I felt an awkwardness within me

That I am not a make of myself but of others;

In other words, I was literally a tabula rasa to others,

Whom I allowed to freely shape me into,

Mold me by, and fill me with their thoughts,

Their whims and fancies, their beliefs, and so on.

I realized I was victimized by such abusive past.

I thought all the complexes and inhibitions

I was endowed with now were the fruits of

My childish behavior of letting others dominate me.

Very sadly, as I reached my adulthood,

I observed my personality as unsteady,

Useless, dithering, and confused.

All my limitations stopped me from climbing up in life status.

I thought going to confession frequently

To lament on my imperfections could change myself.

But I was not growing as an adult

As the world expected of me.

Instead, the same crowd that had brought me

To this wretched condition

Rejoiced, giggled, teased, heaped derision on me;

Sadly, they made sure I wouldn't climb up the ladder of life.

Hence, I blamed everything and everybody around me:

Religion, social networks, philosophies,

Scriptures, and even God. I questioned,

"Where were you, God,

When I was manipulated by humans around me?

You should have come to defend me

And crushed them as a nutcracker."

Within my inner spirit, a loud voice spurred me, saying,

"My dear son, you are playing the role of antagonist

Not only on stage but also in real life.

As any antagonist, you act against yourself and me

On the basis of nonsubstantive evidence.

You make insatiable demands you hold within you.

Undeniably, your dreams are good.

But instead of concentrating yourself on how to realize them

With the talents and opportunities endowed by Me,

You fret over and blame others, including Me.

Remember how I had blessed you through your first parents:

'I entrust every creation to you;

Fill the earth and subdue it' (Gen. 1:28).

I am sorry, because of their sin,

I also ordered you through them:

'In toil you shall eat its yield all the days of your life . . .

By the sweat of your brow you shall eat bread

Until you return to the ground' (Gen. 3:17–19)."

Listening to Him, I did realize my misgivings and mistakes.

I started my journey of sweat and labor, and

Believe me, I lived happily thereafter.

# 51. The Head-Start Faith Formation

In one CNN interview, a mother asked
A famous author, Mr. Neale Donald Walsch,
"When should parents start teaching
Their children about God?" The author retorted,
"When do you start teaching them about love?"
She said, "From their birth."
The author concluded, "So that is it."
I should add, as my personal note,
A child must be introduced to God the Creator
Even from the moment of the baby's conception.
Biologically, there is so much going on
Between the mother and the baby in her womb.
Undoubtedly, this happens in physical dimensions,
And so it is in the spiritual realm too.
The mother, who carries the baby, as well as
The father, who is the baby's conception partner,
Must be spiritually involved
With the baby growing within the womb
In all kinds of spiritual and religious practices,
Especially touching the baby every day
Through their blessing hands and prayers.

# 52. True Faith Is Not to Be Stiff-Necked

As we get older, we want to take pride in saying,

"I always stand by my guns."

To be resolute in our opinion or belief is not bad.

Actually, God commands us to be so in loving Him:

"Love the Lord your God

With your whole heart, with your whole mind,

With your whole soul and with your whole strength."

But how far can it be in the issue of faith?

To start with, our Master never wants us

To be obsessively fixed on religious holdings

As our forebears have upheld erroneous conceptions

Of bourgeois liberalism,

Of Marxist utopianism,

Of aristocratic capitalism,

Similar to those whom Christ has castigated in His day.

Rather, He has demanded us to

Resolutely stick to His Gospel values:

To love and serve the Triune God,

To follow His way of truth to attain eternal life,

To practice a religion of humility and poverty,

Namely, depending on God and caring for the poor.

Sadly, humans' continuous error is
To interpret such holistic demands
With self-centered strings attached
And to lead a hypocritical and puffed-up life. Thus,
They end up in a disastrous fall into the pit of Hell.
Therefore, God never missed any chance
Of reprimanding such "stiff-necked" people.
Opposite to stiff-neckedness is to be levelheaded.
It means to walk tall and with head held high
But possessing a humble and simple spirit within us.
As one preacher underlines it beautifully,
"We should deal with all our religious holdings,
Especially about First and Ultimate Things
Not by the ignorance of the mind
But by the disappearance of the pride of the heart."

# 53. We Walk with Glory but with Caution

Undoubtedly, with no dispute whatsoever,

We can pride ourselves as

The greatest ones in God's creations.

This is what King David sings in Psalm 8:

"You have made human little less than a god,

Crowned him with glory and honor."

Biblical scholars interpret the term "god"

As God creating human beings almost

At the level of the beings in the heavenly world.

In talking about the "recreation"

Done by the Word incarnate,

Some church fathers claim splendidly,

"The divine became human

So that the human can become divine."

And John the Evangelist emphasizes that

The Word that has become flesh

Has given us the power to become children of God, and

"From His fullness we have all

Received grace in place of grace."

By our belief in incarnation,

We are not slaves subjected to the law;

But as God's children,

We inherit an amazing share of

The heavenly Father's power.

As St. Irenaeus predicts,

"We are able to receive greater glory from God."

Consequently,

We are now like stars in the night sky

Shining with clarity of our destiny,

Fishes that swim and rest deep

In the divine mystery of love.

Nonetheless, there is one more fact

We should keep in mind:

Unless we abide in the incarnate Word,

We become small, and our life has little meaning;

Without the Word, we remain

Little people living little lives. This is why

Paul exhorts us (Phil. 2:12),

"Work out your salvation with fear and trembling."

Blessed are we if we,

Without being puffed up but filled with humility,

Persevere in God's love and

In obedience and gratitude to Him.

# SECTION III

# THE QUICKDATA OF GOLDEN AGE

# 54. What Is My Life after All?

According to an author, life is

A concise and complex amalgam of compromises.

From the animal kingdom, we learn

That life depends both on its death

And on its continuity as well.

As we read in scriptures (Eccles. 3:1–8),

Our life is a bundle of

Already designed and appointed times:

Time to give birth, time to die;

Time to plant and time to uproot the plant;

Time to kill, time to heal;

Time to tear down, time to build;

Time to weep, time to laugh;

Time to mourn, time to dance;

Time to scatter stones, time to gather them;

Time to embrace, time to be far from it;

Time to seek, time to lose;

Time to keep, time to cast away;

Time to rend, time to sew;

Time to be silent and time to speak;

Time to love and time to hate;

Time of war and time of peace.

Reviewing my past life game, I know

All humans are destined for

Disintegration and disappearance

As inevitable consequences of our human birth.

The *comedy of life* is

We go on surviving largely by

Ignorance, a blissful satisfaction;

Forgetfulness, a grace-filled inability;

Hopes, dreams, fairy tales.

And thus, we feel restful and satisfied,

But *the tragedy of life* is

Numerous conflicts strangle this peaceful life:

Knowledge, which people label as power;

Consciousness, which is esteemed

As the criterion of being human;

Control from the fittest;

Dependence as social beings;

Freedom, which is interpreted

As the symbol of human maturity.

This doesn't mean

I should be confused or discouraged.

In the past, I have been considering my life as

Some sort of mystery, gambling, and ministry.

But when I have reached my golden age,

I view it differently:

My life is Christ's life, alter Christus.

I still march on happily with this Pauline thought:

"I live, no longer I, but Christ lives in me."

# 55. We Are Sinners . . . but Not Forever

John candidly argues (1 John 1:8–10),

"If we say, 'We are without sin,' we are liars;

If we say, 'We have not sinned,'

We make God a liar."

I don't deny his statements.

However, if we read the entire NT books, we find

If we deny God has forgiven all our sins

By His Son's death,

We then become hybrids of evil

Under the spell of anathemas.

As its follow-up, all that we hear

About the redemptive deeds of God

Written in the Bible and taught by the church

Turn out to be a fairy tale and deceptive vogue.

Just as we are definitely bundles of numerous sins,

So we are definitely forgiven and

Washed clean by the blood of Christ.

Even if we time and again stray away

From our holy path,

Jesus, the Good Shepherd, comes

In search of us and saves us;

Even when we tightly close our inner door,

The same Friend continuously knocks at

And waits for our welcome.

One of the golden-agers I have come across in my life

Has been suffering by memory loss

But never forgets one matter.

He repeats it to any priest loudly:

"I am a bad boy." With that guilt complex,

He avoids partaking in the Holy Communion.

This is why Pope Francis, in a homily, says,

"God's constant invitation is

'Comfort, comfort, comfort my people,'

But we are attached to a spiritual pessimism,"

Undeniably, it is the biblical truth:

God comforts as a mother, even more than her,

Caressing all golden-agers like me

And calming us with TLC words: "Be consoled.

I am your God, and you are My people.

I am with you till the end of

Your golden age in this world."

# 56. Unloading Unnecessary and Unwanted Yokes

To attach to even a tiny, little goal of winning,

We are propelled to detach ourselves

From a few likings of our own.

If that goal is so great as attaining eternal life,

How much more then will we be expected of?

Eternal life, in the light of Jesus, is

An uninterrupted life of bliss, life of true freedom,

Life of peace, and life of full contentment.

To reach such goal in our life,

Being obsessed by it

As if an indescribable treasure (Matt. 13:44–46),

We glue it to our mind and heart

As the priority goal of life (Matt. 6:33)

And go for it, breathe for it, and

Deny every other thing to possess it.

In that hunting process, a spiritual strategy

Is offered from heaven—

To detach ourselves from

Unwanted elements, burdens,

And clutches or strings attached that

Obstruct our path of pursuing the precious goal.

We can call it

Getting rid of those monkeys from our back.

It sounds like an old saying:

"To burn one's bridges behind one."

In the Bible, we read that it is

What the messengers of God and His Son have done:

"Elisha, taking the yoke of oxen, slaughtered them.

He used plowing equipment for fuel to boil the flesh

And gave it to the people to eat. Then he left

And followed Elijah to serve him" (1 Kings 19:21).

So do all Jesus's disciples;

They have left everything they have possessed,

Sold everything they have procured,

Distributed them to the poor,

And then followed Jesus to covet the eternal treasure.

Knowingly or unknowingly,

Many monkeys have been placed

On our back by society and its culture.

They are nuisances many a time,

A kind of large yoke to be borne.

Yet we once have felt we need them.

But Jesus wants us to get rid of them

Totally and completely for the sake of
Entering His heavenly treasure island.
There is some more time
Bestowed to golden-agers
To get rid of unwanted yokes.
Let us instead take up Jesus's yoke
To realize our ultimate goal.
"My yoke is easy, and my burden light" (Matt. 11:30).

# 57. Important Matter to Be Done before Our "Sunset"

I often dictate to my computer

Some of my thoughts to get written.

Sometimes because of my foreign accent,

It will interpret my words wrongly and amuse me.

Once when I dictated,

"Jesus said we should *love our enemies*,"

My computer wrote, "We should *laugh at our enemies*."

This is how some do

Regarding those whom we don't like or hate.

Many others keep on

Their grudge and resentment against enemies;

Thus, as psychologists verify, we lose our restful sleep

And even get ulcers and other complications in the body.

Certainly, love for enemies

Seems madness to common reason.

Upon seeing so much evil in the world,

Especially when that evil affects us deeply,

Our reaction is always anger and perhaps revenge.

But Jesus exhorts us (Matt. 5:44),

"I say to you, love your enemies,

And pray for those who persecute you."

He tells us not to let evil coerce us

To fight it with its own weapons of evil.

His recommendation is to fight it with the weapons of God:

Mercy, forgiveness, and good deeds

As He does through His sun and rain (Matt. 5:45).

Jesus's advice is so relevant and pertinent,

Specially in the life of golden-agers.

Listing the rules for our new life in Christ (Eph. 4:25–32),

Paul underlines the impending need of

Getting rid of anger and revenge.

"Be angry but do not sin;

Do not let the sun set on your anger,

And do not leave room for the devil" (NABRE).

"Do not let resentment lead you into sin;

The sunset must not find you still angry.

Do not give the devil his opportunity" (Jerusalem Bible).

My personal entry here is

Every golden-ager willy-nilly is enjoying the sunset of life.

I consider seriously what Paul pinpoints,

Not just the daily sunset but also the sunset of life.

Forgiving and blessing our enemies is

More important at the sunset of our life than ever before

Because we are getting closer

To our Creator and Redeemer;

Plus, because of God's immense love,

We are fortunately granted to live the golden age

As His gratuitous gift of "grace time"

To be holier, to be more merciful,

And to reciprocate His Love.

Let us make the maximum use of this precious grace time

To remove from us all bitterness, fury,

Anger, shouting, and reviling

But to be kind and compassionate to one another

And forgiving one another

As God has forgiven us in Christ.

This is the only way to make our sunset more beautiful.

# 58. Blessed Is Our Human Body

From my childhood, I have been taught to be very cautious
In my dealings with three enemies to my spiritual life:
World, devil, and body.
Undoubtedly, as the Bible states,
Our life on the earth is a war zone
Between the evil and the good
In which every step of our march to the goal of good life
Is being tested through wounds caused by evil.
Evil is personified but acts out in three forces:
First is the world, the value system (James 4:4)
That is totally contrary to the ways of God
And acts as an exterior force subjecting us to worldliness.
"To be a friend of the world is to be an enemy of God."
Second is the devil, a shrewd fallen angel,
Invisible and subtle,
A spiritual adversary prowling around like a roaring lion,
Seeking someone to devour (1 Pet. 5:8–9).
Third, the body, a clay pot created by God
To be a fitting mansion
To store His image and likeness in the form of soul,
Is also considered to be an adversary in our spiritual life.

In the light of Christ, I claim it is a wrong view.

Our body is indeed a biological fabric

Made of inner and outer organs,

Blood, bones, skin, and so on.

It is a sleeping but fading beauty designed by the Creator.

According to the two-thousand-year-old Christian belief,

God has appeared to the world in a human body.

The divine Supreme has taken a physical body

As His own dwelling.

When Jesus has come into the world,

He has willingly embraced that body

Because He believes it is His Father's will.

"Sacrifice you did not desire,

But a body you prepared for me" (Heb. 10:5).

Hence, the term "body" taken as an enemy

Must have a different connotation.

In the words of Paul, it says the "flesh," as inner foe,

Is our human nature with its natural tendency to sin.

It is our inner foe, a self-centered personality.

Paul calls it the "old man."

But our visible and vulnerable body is a wonderful device,

Blessed and remodeled by the incarnate Word

And entrusted to golden-agers by God for many decades,

Despite our vulnerability, sinfulness, and corruptibility.

Because of His mysterious deed,

It has been cleansed, medicated.

Even if we suffer pains and pitfalls because of it,

They become a part of the redemptive action of the Lord.

This is why Paul exhorts us,

"By the mercies of God,

To offer your bodies as a living sacrifice,

Holy and pleasing to God, your spiritual worship" (Rom. 12:1).

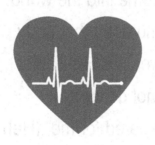

# 59. My Romantic Eventide Song

When every evening arrives, nature bugles,

"The day is done."

As the sun, which arises

And travels through the sky, sets down,

We encounter bleak gloom surreally encircling us.

This sort of watershed consciousness

May whoop us stridently when we reach the golden age.

The daytime of our life is gone; we enter into its eventide.

But a sensible and honorable person considers differently:

Yes, the day may be done, the sun may set down,

The night may envelope around. Even the moonflower

May not sprinkle its white petals on us.

But God's grace, being the divine sun,

Never sets and never sheds its brightness.

Yes, dusk of isolation may descend over us,

The shadows of disabilities may fall upon us,

And awful misery and unhappiness may snoop within us.

But God's unfailing, ever-abiding love

Never will abandon us, the rebellious renegades.

After all, our golden age is not a period of decline;

Rather, it is a time of declaring firmly,

"God loves me as I am."

It is a precious moment to inscribe within the inner spirit

"I will always uphold

Staunch faith in my Supreme Master.

I will never lose

Relentless hope in my compassionate Redeemer.

I will ever keep on musing and singing

A melodious song—

It is indeed a love song—

To my one and only Lover, my heavenly Bridegroom."

# 60. The Spirit's Engagements with Golden-Agers

I had come across so many golden-agers

Anointed by God's Spirit.

I witnessed in them how

He had been working in them in different ways.

Just as they were interiorly directed by the Spirit,

So were their outward actions and reactions.

Occasionally being on fire, urged by caritas,

They were shedding tears over their fellow humans,

Praying constantly for their own family members,

Their communities, and the entire human race.

Very often I observed them embracing everyone they met

Without any discrimination, good and bad alike.

Every now and then, I was stunned to notice

Their lowliness of spirit, esteeming themselves as the

lowest and most miserable creature among all mankind.

Periodically, I found them literally seized by the Spirit,

Moving around in wheelchairs or lying on the clinical bed

In indefinable joy as jolly, good fellows.

Whenever an occasion arose to debate about

Certain apologetics of faith,

Some golden-agers, baptized in the Spirit,

Demonstrated themselves as the knights of Jesus

In defending the true faith bravely.

Off and on, many of them were restful

In the deepest silence

Generated from their Spirit-filled inner state of relaxation,

Accepting well their blissful existence.

Thus, I understood from them the indescribable ways

The Spirit's grace works within golden-agers

And thus how the Spirit prepares every golden-ager

To stand one day before the heavenly Father

Pure, whole, and blameless.

# 61. Golden-Agers' Waiting: Passive or Active?

Life is treated as a voyage, a travel, a pilgrimage.

The core component that makes this trip a typical one is

Waiting and longing to reach the destination of it.

Truly, golden-agers' waiting as Christians is

For the "total fulfillment" at the Second Coming of Christ.

I should not stop there.

I should go beyond this fact and conclude that

This Parousia waiting in golden age means

Being more aware of

What I am and

What I possess already.

In this process,

I totally agree with Paul asserting (1 Cor. 1:7)

I am not lacking in any spiritual gifts as I wait.

I therefore don't wait for the receiving of the gifts.

Nevertheless, I listen humbly to the advice of God in Jesus:

Awake—"Be aware."

Recognize—"Be conscious."

Serve in alertness "His people until the Master returns"

With the maximum use of what I already possess.

# 62. God's Amazing Promises to Golden-Agers

It is said, plus proved,

That as we grow older, we are deprived of sharp memory

About our past and present,

About the names, the places,

And the relationships we are acquainted with.

However, I believe with my short experience of life

That humans who have wholeheartedly

Surrendered to the divine

Never lose sight

Of the loving promises of God for His children,

Especially His astounding promises

To humans, divinity;

To mortals, immortality;

To sinners, justification; and

To the poor, a rising to glory.

These multiple promises are beautifully

Summed up by St. Augustine:

"It is nothing but eternal salvation;

Everlasting happiness with the angels;

An immortal inheritance; endless glory;

Joyful vision of God's face;

Dwelling in his holy dwelling in heaven;

And after resurrection from the dead no further fear of dying."

How can it be possible that God permits

Such ineffable promises to be forgotten by the golden-agers,

Who are continuously thinking, believing, and hoping

Those promises about eternal life

As their one and only goal of all their striving in this world?

Never—I say it again, *never.*

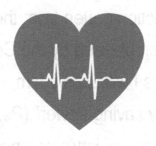

# 63. Brightness and Bleakness of Seniority

Though the word "seniority" comes from the term "senior,"

Commonly, "senior" refers to the years a person has lived,

But "seniority"—used mostly

In an organizational environment—

Suggests the length of years a person has served.

In both cases, we find brightness and bleakness.

The brightness in seniors' life comes

Only by their conviction gotten from the Scriptures—

That they have been blessed by the Creator:

"With length of days I will satisfy him,

And fill him with my saving power" (Ps. 91:16).

And from enlightened society's perspective,

Seniors' wisdom guides the next generation;

Their sharing of experiences cautions young ones.

Their warmth and concern heals the afflicted.

Above all, their relentless faith and prayer strengthens us.

Regarding the brightness in seniority stage,

It can bring a privileged status in their workplaces,

Which usually determines

The order of promotion and benefits.

As for the bleakness in both situations,

So many seniors may not feel they are blessing to others

Either because of the ingratitude and coldness of people

Or because of their own carelessness to God's admonition:

"Gray-headedness is a crown of beauty

When it is found in the way of righteousness" (Prov. 16:31).

"Better is a poor but wise youth than an old but foolish king who no longer knows caution" (Eccles. 4:13).

As for those most senior in job situations,

Their future will become unpredictable because

Their life is totally dependent on

The future of the company or institution.

There is fear and tension about layoffs or early retirement.

In all the cases listed above,

Blessed is the golden-ager who lisps daily to God,

"Now that I am old and gray,

Do not forsake me, God,

That I may proclaim your might

To all generations yet to come" (Ps. 71:18).

# 64. It Takes Unique Faith To Live to One Hundred and Beyond

"If we're hoping to live to hundreds,

We need to watch more than our diet,"

Writes Carol Marak in her essay on the study of aging.

She is right in her assessment. Studies declare so:

"Living our golden age to more than one hundred years

Is not the sunny climate or fat-free, gluten-free diet

Rather, certain psychological set of attitudes."

Secular writers may call it

A stubborn and resilient mind-set.

In the light of our scriptures, we can name it chutzpah.

This Hebrew term means

A supreme self-confidence, a shameless audacity,

An impudent nerve, a brazen frame of mind.

All the above-mentioned characteristics may sound natural.

But when the ray of God's light enters through it,

It turns out to be persistent faith that,

Even the size of a mustard seed, produces abundant results.

First, it removes negative feelings and behaviors from us:

Overanxiety, avariciousness, overeating, uncontrolled lust,

Unbridled and unreal ambitions,

Oversensitiveness, and so on.

Second, it fills us with positive thoughts such as

*God in me is powerful. He is all-good, trustworthy.*

*He takes care of me. Why and whom should I fear?*

*It makes me humble and meek,*

*Develops a spiritual stamina within me.*

*It begets wisdom in me to manage properly*

*My health, wealth, and self.*

*I become a daredevil in tough situations such as*

*Depression, ailments, rejection, and loss of loved ones.*

This is why our Master has repeatedly said

When the sick have been cured,

"Your chutzpah has saved you."

Blessed are the friends who possess such chutzpah spirit;

Certainly, they will see one hundred and beyond.

# 65. Mysterious Plan of Christ for Golden-Agers

In the Christian belief,

"God's mysteries were fulfilled in Christ.

St. John Eudes writes

In his book on the kingdom of Jesus:

"While all God's mysteries are complete

In the person of Jesus

It is not yet in us, the members of his mystical Body.

He, as risen Lord, continues to fulfill the same in us,

Even today. He wants to give us a share in them and

To accomplish and continue them in us."

In this, we know well

Jesus expects our voluntary cooperation.

First, we should express our sincere longing for it by praying,

"Father, let your kingdom come," and

"Let your will be done on earth as it is in heaven."

Second, He fills us with the needed grace

Through His sacraments and other church practices.

Third, He demands from us to take up the cross

Of our bodily and psychological sufferings,

Through which He has brought glory to His Father

And effected salvation in humans.

Paul understands this demand of the risen Lord

And joyfully states (Col. 1:24),

"Now I rejoice in my sufferings for your sake, and in my flesh

I am filling up what is lacking in the afflictions of Christ."

Christ completes God's plan

In accordance with our life span and life situation.

Those of us who have attained our golden age

Are truly blessed because

Both the Father and His Son have specially chosen us

To have a long life, which indeed comes with

Too many physical, mental, and social problems.

But we are thrice blessed, becoming Christ's favorites

In cooperating with Him, taking golden age crosses

To bring God's plan of salvation to fulfillment

In our family, community, and

Certainly the entire global humanity.

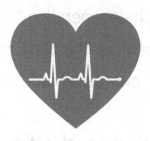

# 66. Golden Assessment of Golden-Agers by the Pope

In his weekly audience (as published in CNS, March 4, 2015),

Pope Francis declared to the world,

Especially to the youngsters,

"The aged are the reserve of the wisdom of our people;

They have experienced and survived the struggles

To raise a family and provide them with a dignified life.

Tossing them aside means

Tossing aside their experience

And the way that experience can contribute

To making life better today."

He too added, "A society

That cannot show gratitude and affection

To the elderly is a perverse society.

The church, faithful to the word of God,

Cannot tolerate such degeneration."

And with full enforcement, the pope concluded,

"Seeing the elderly, only as a burden, is ugly.

It's a mortal sin."

Wow, what a marvelous papal testimony

On the dignity of golden-agers.

# 67. In Pursuit of Abundant Life

All golden-agers know well that,

Both for our survival and development,

We perform two basic actions:

Attachment to a goal, which are mostly short term,

And detachment from all that

Obstruct us from achieving that goal.

But to lead and attain a self-fulfilling

And soul-enriching life of joy, which Jesus calls

The abundant life, is indeed a long-term goal.

To realize this goal,

As any goal-achieving effort demands,

We need to discover our goal and fix it to our mind and heart.

Jesus says,

"First seek the kingdom of God" (Matt. 13:44–46).

He exhorts us to esteem this goal

As the most precious treasure.

Once we find it, we are to put our heart into it,

Namely, to possess an obsession toward it wholeheartedly,

With our whole mind, whole soul, and whole strength.

In the resolute pursuit of eternal life as our goal,

Jesus recommends also to detach ourselves

From any unwanted elements
That are obstructing our path.
We can call this action
As getting rid of those monkeys from our back.
The old sayings are
"Burn one's bridges behind one" and "Burn one's boats."
It means to embark on a certain course of action
From which it becomes impossible to return.
This is what Jesus commands us
Who are committed to achieve eternal life:
"Leave everything and follow me."
Paul expounds this golden saying of Jesus (Gal. 5:1):
"For freedom Christ set us free;
So stand firm and do not submit again to the yoke of slavery."
Attainment of the abundant eternal life
Indeed calls for commitment and freedom,
Which may seem quite incompatible for some.
Yet Jesus calls us for this total commitment in total freedom.
Once we are acquainted with Christ daily in this spirit,
We will be able to assert with Paul,
"One thing I do, forgetting what lies behind
And straining forward to what lies ahead,
I press on toward the goal for the prize
Of the upward call of God in Christ Jesus!" (Phil. 3:13–14).

# 68. The Flip-Flap of My Heartbeat: Die before I Die

When I attained my "muddle age" (sixty-five and over),

My heart was beating, *I want to die before I die.*

It was due to the burden of my body's wear and tear,

Plus a sort of psychological trauma of

Losing my public extravaganza by retirement.

I felt awkward to be esteemed by society

As "useless to the world."

Besides, I became overanxious about my future

Of the tingling and crippled phase of assisted living.

I already felt that the symptoms of life's downfall

That I listed above had been starting even from my youth:

I confronted my baldness at twenty-five.

At "doggy year," forty, I had to wear reading glasses.

At age fifty-five, I was diagnosed with type 2 diabetes.

Even at sixty, my "countable" hair was becoming totally gray.

Thus, at age sixty-eight,

The nightfall of old age was upsetting me.

Despite my clear understanding that

Such changes in my body were only inevitable,

I hated them to ride herd on my youthful spirit,

And I longed to die in the same exuberant spirit
I tried to retain.
I thought I may lose this vibrant spirit by body degeneration
Before the final curtain of my life drama fell on me.
However, as the last but one scene of my life, at age seventy,
The realistic curtain opened; I discovered
The exuberant spirit I upheld for years *in faith and hope*
Would stay unimpaired even after seventy
In the midst of all the bodily life's rocky sunset games,
Which the poet Yeats describes:
"Where all the ladders end; in the foul rag
And bone shop of encroaching decrepitude."
So I know now why this age, seventy and over, is named as
The golden age.

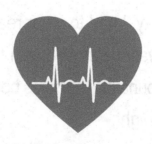

# 69. Golden Age in the Eyes of God

As Paul writes in Romans 12:1,

Every Christian must offer our bodies as a living sacrifice,

Holy and pleasing to God, as our spiritual worship.

The most appropriate time of offering

Such auspicious sacrifice is none other

Than the golden age.

"God approves sacrifices

Of the afflicted persons" (Isa. 66:1–2).

After knowing supremely well God's desire,

Jesus says to God (Heb. 10:5–7),

"Sacrifices you did not desire,

But a body you prepared for me . . .

Then I said . . . behold, I come to do your will, O God."

I have read God's preference of a living sacrifice;

I have tried my best to work at it; I swear,

I have failed and failed.

A beautiful time has come;

People have labeled me as old.

I too have realized it slowly but hesitantly.

Lately, I understand why the Lord has offered His body

And taken pride in it as a living sacrifice that pleases God.

I begin to make it as my daily offering:

In this sacrifice basket, I have offered

My own physical ailment, my disabilities,

My mental frustration and doubts,

My spiritual vacuum that I have

Been careless about for years,

Plus a little bit of faith, hope, and charity,

Toward my Triune God.

It is indeed a genuine living sacrifice;

Truly, it is "actual" and not just "ritual."

Bedridden? No problem; my sickbed is the altar.

Wheelchaired? Not an issue;

It is the sanctuary my Master likes.

That is because

Wherever I am thrown into, because of my oldness,

My heart beats always,

*Here I am, Lord. I come to do Your will.*

Is it not my golden age, a precious time gift from God?

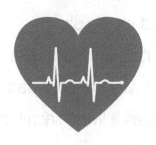

# 70. Golden Age Doesn't Frighten but Brightens Me

As I journey to cross the threshold of the final station,

My brain stands under the bright sun;

It reminds me how I have lived a dishonest life.

I have brought disruption in the peaceful life of some

Using the colonial tactic of "divide and govern,"

Cheating myself, saying, "It is sheer diplomacy."

I have said yes many times instead of no

And other times said no instead of yes,

Deceiving myself, saying, "They are mere white lies."

I have been a mudslinger to many

To tarnish their reputation and good name

In my avid desire of climbing up life's ladder,

Conning myself, saying, "It is a survival technique."

In prayer, even I dare enough to challenge the Lord—

"You have tested my heart, searched it in the night.

You have tried me by fire,

But find no malice in me" (Ps. 17)—

Duping myself, saying, "God is a goody-goody Abba."

At this age, I understand clearly that

All the above listed and more

Are very offensive to the Triune God;

I feel before Him like "nothing but a piece of ass."

Instantaneously, I also hear Him saying to me,

"Well, I guess you see where this is going.

It is good to know that you realize what you have been.

But I tell you I still love you.

I cannot but love you. You are everything to me."

Let me stand under the shadow of His wings of mercy;

Let me walk in hope that the time is nearing.

An immense reward is waiting for me.

# 71. The Christened Heartbeats of Golden-Agers

Since death is ever near at hand

Through the inescapable necessity of nature,

Many men and women—after living and breathing

That their salvation is from Jesus,

At the sunset of their life,

Despite its bitter consequences—

Consider it a blessing to embrace it

And thus to gain the reward of eternal life.

Hence, the apostle Paul rightly declares,

"You have been granted the privilege

Not only to believe in Christ

But also to suffer for his sake."

He affirms such suffering

Is Christ's gift for the chosen one;

The sufferings of this present time are not worthy

To be compared with the glory that is to be revealed in us.

Yes, the righteous have exhorted themselves night and day:

"In the view of the foolish, we may seem to be dead;

And our passing away may be thought an affliction;

But we are in peace;

Chastised a little, we shall be greatly blessed;

Because we affirm:

God's grace and mercy are with his holy ones,

And his care is with the elect" (Ws 3:1–9).

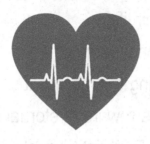

# 72. Living in Spirit and in Fire

In our golden age, most of us take "freelance liberty" of

Nostalgic thinking and bragging about

All that we have accomplished in the past

And find some satisfaction in it.

I partially agree on the usability of this imaginative pleasure.

Through my natural IQ, through my DNA,

Through my natural talents and my diplomatic intelligence,

I have amassed possessions, qualifications,

So many friends, and so on. However, I know

They were sheer natural fruits from natural roots.

I come to an understanding as I have started my golden age

That mere fleshly and imaginative clinging to my natural fruits

Is not making them stay evergreen

Within me to offer satisfaction,

Nor do the people around me relish hearing my bragging

As sounding like an old and cracked gramophone record.

More specially, in the light of God's Word, I am enlightened

These natural fruits won't offer me now any godly blessings

Of inner strength, greater hope, and remarkable serenity.

Therefore, our Master recommends

To His disciples, like me,

It needs more than the baptism of water.

We need to be baptized in spirit and in fire, meaning,

To drink fully God's living waters,

To dive deeply into His spiritual ocean,

To be truly "influenced" by His Spirit,

And to be refined by His fire.

Without such experiences, none of us can be

Righteous, holy, and merciful as God is

To be a faithful child of God as Jesus

And to face chivalrously our golden age upshots—

Illness, pain, uselessness, frustration, and so on—

With the brightest view that

All of them are designed by God

To refine our "raw" golden age in His fire of love

Into the purest and most valuable period we have ever lived.

Thus, our longest enduring life on the earth

Will prove to become a source of inheriting

Praise, glory, and honor in the coming day of Christ.

# 73. Discerning the Signs of the Times

By experience and by the Bible,

The golden-agers are esteemed as "persons of wisdom."

The fact of how accurate this assessment is

Largely depends on how we judge

The happenings in and around us.

Regarding the significant signs filling the globe around us,

Our Master says in Matthew 16:3 and Luke 12:56

To rebuke His enemies who are able to read

The indications of the coming weather or present time

But not the indications of the coming of God's kingdom.

Indeed, He points out the deplorable events happening

Both in His time and in the future

As negative signs for God's kingdom

*Not yet* fully established.

At the same time, He says His mighty deeds and teachings

Are positive signs of God's kingdom *already* come.

Regarding the considerable signs within our life,

Our past accomplishments if they are fairly judged,

They clarify that God's kingdom

Has been established *already*

Through sacraments but *not yet* fully grown within us.

As for the present life in the period of our golden age,

Though God in Jesus has designed

Abundant chances *already*

To build up within us His kingdom of peace and joy,

If we are honest to ourselves, we will accept that

His kingdom has *not yet* become part and parcel of our life;

We are indeed careless, we resist,

And we are not attuned to His will.

Reading clearly these signs of our times—

Already but not yet—

Let us wake up, let us rise,

Let us embrace willingly the precious time of golden age

With all its bittersweet consequences.

# 74. The Silvery Widows in the Glowing Eyes of God

Astonishingly, we find eighty direct references

About widows in the scriptures, both in OT and NT.

The Word of God emphasizes elaborately that

God is the compassionate defender of widows. He is

"Father of the fatherless, defender of widows" (Ps. 68).

To imitate Him in protecting widows in communities and

To forbid us to take advantage of their vulnerability,

God has exclusively formulated certain social laws such as

"You shall not wrong any widow" (Exod. 22:21),

And He wanted us to be diligent about not isolating them:

"Include the widows in all your festivals" (Deut. 16:11–14).

Jesus, God's Son, has imitated His Father

In respecting and honoring every widow in His life.

He knows their sufferings; His care for them is expressed

By offering support to them as He has done for His mother

By His miracle of raising a dead son (Luke 7:11–17)

And returning him to his widowed mother at Nain.

He condemns the mistreatment of widows (Matt. 23:24).

The church community, from its early stage (Acts 6:1–7),

Continues till this day the same services for the widows.

Paul (1 Tim. 5:3–16) and James (1:27)

Instruct Christians about this remarkable service.

Therefore,

To you, my dear golden-aged widows,

Wherever you are, whatever you struggle with,

Kindly remember two adages

That must hover over you with sunshine:

"You are a favorite of God."

"You are indeed a blessing to today's world."

As David Lloyd George has once asserted,

"The true test of a civilization is

The way it treats its old people."

# 75. I Am Lifted from Muddy Waters

The story about my earthly life

Can be divided into six sections:

Section 1. I started my life floating in

A sac (womb) of amniotic fluid;

I was safely and securely floating and moving in that fluid.

It was a cozy air-conditioned, cushionlike place

Free of bumps and injury.

Section 2. A period of walking unsteadily but not knowing

Those years were the most important time

In my cognitive, emotional, and social development.

Section 3. I call this period of my life "youth": It included

Teenage, adolescence, and even a few years of adulthood.

People may claim it as

The most dangerous and the riskiest time. As for me,

I felt like moving within the safety network of faith.

I disliked it, but I couldn't do anything.

One thing I was blessed with was

I was not put in public jail for any public sin.

In private, I did risky businesses of testing my maleness;

Constantly, I uttered bitter words against authorities.

Section 4. With the effects of the previous period,

I entered middle age, where I was offered a unique chance
To breathe freedom and act out my glorious independence.
Section 5. I fondly call this period "muddle age."
I was feeling like the psalmist (Ps. 69):
"The waters have risen to my neck.
I have sunk into the mud of the deep
And there is no foothold. The waves overwhelm me."
I too lodged lots of complaints before the just God
Except, in few things, I never disowned the Lord;
Indeed, I made many attempts to get away from His grip,
But they were sort of crazy, lucid intervals.
Section 6. This is where I am now, the golden age.
The good Lord is sharing with me
Not only more of His wisdom and truth
To understand His unending compassion for me
But also more of His graceful stamina
To put up with my aged body.
As the psalmist testifies,
I am truly lifted from my
Muddy waters.

# 76. Spectacular Breakthrough by a Last-Ditch Effort

In my seminary days, as a young man of twenty,

I had been struggling with my guilty conscience

About my imperfections in performing my duties,

Plus about my inability to control sexual temptations.

Discussing with spiritual mentors in counseling, I tried

To get some effective solutions to erase my guilty feelings,

But all they offered were these:

-Temptations are inevitable.

-Perhaps most of them will disappear

When you get old (golden age).

-As most of us do, consider the burden

You feel as one of your crosses.

-Daily surrender yourself to God with your crosses smilingly.

As a matter of fact, I was not satisfied with their counsels.

The years went on, and the struggle continued,

sometimes more intensely.

Leaving God's amazing powerful hands, at my middle age,

I made a desperate attempt to get some human consolation,

Which I thought would cure

The inner wounds of my long struggle.

I swear, my struggle became enlarged

From emotional to spiritual.

Soon I decided to come out of all human help because

They might have been genuine

But had their side effects as pills did.

Already, I reached my "muddle age,"

Where—as my mentors prophesied—

I felt a few of my temptations going away,

Maybe because of my oldness,

But not my guilty feeling

Of not performing my duties purely

To please the Lord and for His great glory but

Performing everything for my own glory and appreciation.

By then, I reached the door of golden age,

Which was, as God's Word and human experience dictated,

The last but one station before reaching my ultimate destiny.

Hence, I collected and recollected all biblical messages

And decided to make a last-ditch effort,

As military people did,

To fix my wrong, self-centered life and ministry.

My Master redirected me to my former mentors

To reread their counsel: surrender to the Almighty willfully

All your anxiety to be perfect

And your inability to realize it.

To get acquainted with surrendering, they had said,

"Recite St. Ignatius's morning and evening prayer."

At present, I am persistent in reciting that prayer daily.

It has helped me. My heart is peaceful; my struggle subsided.

Thus, I have gladly joined

The club of many golden-aged friends

Who too have selected the daily prayer

As their last ditch-effort:

"Take and receive, O Lord, my liberty.

Take all my will, my mind, my memory.

Do Thou direct and govern all and sway.

Do what Thou wilt, command, and I obey.

Only Thy grace and love on me bestow.

Possessing these all riches I forgo.

All things I hold and all I won are Thine.

Thine was the gift, to Thee I all resign."

# 77. The Tripod of Golden Age Spirituality

Every just and wise person possesses two prophetic eyes:

One eye sees the wickedness of humans, and

The other sees the goodness of God.

We discover this fact well portrayed in the book of Isaiah,

Especially chapters 51 and 52.

First, he underlines the evils done by God's people:

"You who drank at the Lord's hand the cup of his wrath.

Your misfortunes are double;

Desolation and destruction, famine and sword!

Your sons lie helpless. They are filled with

The wrath of the Lord, the rebuke of your God."

Then immediately, the prophet sees

Also the goodness of the Lord:

"Put on your strength, O Zion; Put on your glorious garments,

Shake off the dust, break out together in song,

See, I am taking from your hand the cup of staggering.

The bowl of my wrath you shall no longer drink.

For the Lord comforts his people, he redeems Jerusalem."

The psalmist joins the prophet

With the same twofold perception (Ps. 73).

Plus, he includes one more insight

About his personal encounter with God.

Like most of us, he portrays

His inner feelings hurt by God's silence,

And then he confesses splendidly

His lowness and God's greatness:

"Since my heart was embittered

And my soul deeply wounded,

I was stupid and . . . I was like a brute beast in your presence.

Yet you take hold of my right hand.

With your counsel you guide me,

And at the end receive me with honor.

Whom else have I in the heavens?

None beside you delights me on earth.

As for me, to be near God is my good,

To make the Lord God my refuge."

We can boldly label such inner perceptions as

The wise tripod of golden age spirituality.

# 78. God about My Golden Age

As most of my colleagues,

When I reached my golden age,

I developed some qualms:

"I am getting old."

I saw my head reaching its peak of bleak baldness.

I noticed the little hair left,

Which demonstrated my dreariness.

I felt awkward as my eyesight became dull and hazy.

Worse still, I frequented the restroom and dental clinic.

In frustration, I questioned,

"Is that all for my faithfulness to the Creator?"

Surprisingly, in one of the regular church prayer times,

I came across a passage

From Isaiah (46:1–13) where God said,

"Hear me, O house of Jacob,

All who remain of the house of Israel!

My burden since your birth,

Whom I have carried from your infancy.

Even to your old age I am the same,

Even when your hair is gray I will bear you;

It is I who have done this,

I who will continue, and I who will carry you to safety."

At that instance, I thought God was speaking to me.

"I am your beginning,

I am your end,

And I continue carrying you in My bosom

Despite the loss of your youth, productivity, and popularity

And most importantly

Despite your becoming a burden and pain to Me."

Then and there, I cried out, like Job,

"Thank you, Lord. I love myself getting old.

Surely, Lord, more than ever before,

Now I am truly a glittering golden person."

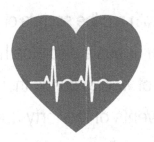

# 79. Looking at Golden Age through Biblical Prism

Whenever I recollect the waiting moments of my life—

Those rush minutes at the traffic jam,

Those ponderous seconds during the surgery of my dad,

Those unbearable moments of waiting to see a friend—

My spinning brain cries out, "Horrible times of my life clock!"

When my mom has reached 90,

She has expressed impatience at living.

However, she has kept her breathing intact and steady till 102.

I have met so many golden-agers with such stalwartness

In their wait to meet the Lord. How is it possible?

Many have shared with me the secrets of a victorious survival.

They point out how Jesus's disciples have managed with

The same difficulty of waiting during their famous "ten days."

Gospels narrate events of the forty days

After Jesus's death and resurrection:

The disciples have seen the risen Lord,

Spoken with Him, And eaten with Him.

Also, before He has ascended

To Heaven on the fortieth day,

They have heard Him ordering them (Luke 24:49),

"Behold I am sending

The promise of my Father upon you;

Stay in the city until you are clothed with power from on high."

He means they must wait for the Spirit for their empowerment.

As Luke tells us, the Spirit has empowered them

After ten days.

It is very interesting to note from the scriptures

How the disciples have handled

Such an anxiety-filled situation.

"They were just devoted to prayer" (Acts 1:14).

This doesn't mean they have been reciting certain prayers

only. They were simply preoccupied with the Lord,

Filled with an earnest desire for His promises to be fulfilled.

They were groaning for His Spirit to come down on them.

Their attitude of prayer was not one of

Using it as a remote control to put God in their direction

And get what they expected from Him.

Rather, there was a deep sense

Of having hopes and dreams

To receive their empowerment from the Spirit.

They were overwhelmed with the sweet memories of

Their days and nights with Jesus

While He had been present.

They remembered the wondrous deeds

He had done among them.

Their lips were praising heartily

His greatness, Love, and mercy.

They were intensely engaged in a prayer of faith

With shameless persistence,

With that "raw nerve" (chutzpah).

They were praying in unity with Jesus's mother and friends:

"Where two or three gathered in my name, I will be there."

They were not loners in praying;

They were encouraging one another,

Interceding for one another in those hectic moments.

They have made it a time of mutual sharing and communion.

Indeed the disciples have changed

Those terrible ten days of darkness

Into a time of intense, loving, and productive prayer.

We should be clear that Jesus has never promised

A ten-day countdown for His promise to be fulfilled.

He had only promised the Spirit.

It was the disciples' devotion to Prayer that has brought

The right fulfillment at the right time.

Golden-agers are obviously living

in the same situation as the Disciples,

waiting to meet the Lord
at their life's finale.
Their long time may be extended to a longer time.
Smarty as they are, they know how *to transform*
*It through prayer as a sweet agony of salvation.*

# 80. Entitled to Bestow God's Blessings

OT books never miss portraying the uniqueness

And efficacy of the blessings showered by Jewish elders,

Specifically the blessing of Jacob, found in Genesis 49,

And the blessing of Moses, read in Deuteronomy 33.

Both have been esteemed for centuries

As prophetic poems

That spell out the words of blessings

Showered by Jacob and Moses to the tribes of Israel

As they are about to leave, living a life full to the brim.

While we find Moses uttering only words of blessing,

Jacob seems to include in his blessings

Curses to some of the tribes.

And the amazing truth is Jewish history proves

That all those words of elders have been realized in full.

Strikingly, the same God

Demands Moses (Num. 6:23–27)

To delegate to other elders the role of

Blessing people with words like

"The Lord bless you and keep you!

The Lord let his face shine upon you,

And be gracious to you!

The Lord look upon you kindly and give you peace!"

And the Lord has promised if they do so,

He will bless the people.

This is a perennial belief in every religious community;

God's intervention in a time in human life

Comes through the words of elders.

God has entrusted

Such wonderful authority and responsibility

To us who are permitted to see our full years.

The golden age is a ripened time for humans to shower

Fruits of blessings to fellow humans as proxies of God.

It is not merely through gestures or a blessing words;

It is also becoming peacemakers, joyful givers,

And strong defenders of justice and truth—

In sum, to be a sunshine in other people's lives.

One important thing we should never forget is

Without willfully making God as our first preference,

Anything we perform or accomplish for others

Will turn out to be more a curse than a blessing.

Let us humbly claim the golden role of blessing

But forcefully stand by God to be effective

Even in our time of insufficient energy and health.

# 81. Golden-Agers Are Gifted with a Third Eye

Many cultures have been underlining

The fact of a third eye

Or inner eye existing within humans.

The Bible refers to it 887 times,

Starting from Genesis (3:5–7).

The Hebrew word for "eyes" is not plural but singular,

Namely, the singular and spectacular "eye of the soul."

Creating humans in His image and

By breathing His Spirit into them,

God has shared with them a certain spiritual ability

To see and probe into the mysteries of their life

And of God.

Besides, NT books also contain many references to it:

"The lamp of the body is the eye. If your eye is sound,

Your whole body will be filled with light" (Matt. 6:22–23).

This inner eye has been highly esteemed

By all spiritual teachers as

A source of knowledge about supernatural powers,

Beyond the range of ordinary senses.

It is also the rarest gift bestowed only by God's Spirit.

This is why Jesus has praised and thanked God

For such a blessing granted to His disciples (Matt. 11:25):

"Although you have hidden these things

From the wise and the learned

You have revealed them to the childlike!"

Seeing through the third eye, therefore, means

As if opening a gate between two worlds:

Inner and outer, surface and depth,

Spiritual and physical, heavenly and earthly.

In our youth and adulthood days,

We might have brushed out completely the term "meditation."

Maybe we have been too busy to look into this

As a sheer waste of time.

Perhaps we have imagined it is only for monks.

But let us never forget

Every one of us is gifted with a precious third eye

Remaining silently, breathing the fresh air slowly and gently,

Sitting somewhere or even riding in a wheelchair,

Or lying in bed, not ridden but in solitude,

Thinking, reflecting, and talking to the Soul King, God,

All by ourselves, alone with Him. I tell you,

It is something that we can do and enjoy

With no cost whatsoever, except giving thanks to God

For letting us have more time and a greater opportunity

And for carrying more matters to discuss with Him

Spirit to spirit, face-to-face, and most of all eye to eye.

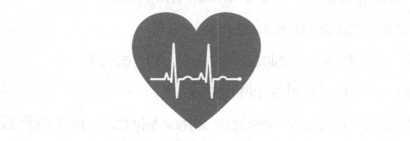

# 82. Leading an Honorable Life Now More Than Ever

As we get into the golden age,

We regret that we are not as busy as before.

But Søren A. Kierkegaard, a religious author, writes,

"To be busy is only a decision but

All that matters is our presence

That is more rewarding than productivity.

By being busy we actually

Conspire to be absent from ourselves!"

We too wrongly quote the scriptures to augment it.

Indeed, Jesus exhorts us to be active

As faithful servants (Mark 13:32–37).

"Be watchful. Be alert," He says and also offers a valid reason:

"You do not know when the lord of the house is coming,

Whether in the evening, or at midnight,

Or at cockcrow, or in the Morning.

May he not come suddenly

And find you sleeping!"

And Paul and the apostles preach about the same message.

However, these biblical thoughts

Direct every disciple of Christ who moves and breathes

In this eschatological time,

Between His first coming and the second,

To walk the walk of Jesus day in and day out and

To move and live daily in sincerity of heart and mind.

They never induce us to be busy with many earthly things

That make us forget ourselves and our destiny,

A "golden" purpose for which

God has offered a "golden" chance.

Yes, we should not stop

Performing good works within our ability.

Yes, we should spend

More time in prayer than self-gratification.

Yes, we should plead constantly

For forgiveness and mercy for us and for our friends.

Yes, we should patiently carry

The yoke of bodily ailments as and with the crucified Jesus.

And believe me, our time is up, friends.

This is what Jesus and His apostles love

To see in golden-agers:

"Put on the armor of light. Let us live honorably as in the day

You know the time in which we are living;

It is the hour now for you to awake from sleep.

For our salvation is nearer now

Than when we first believed" (Rom. 13).

# 83. Golden Time for True Conversion

In church history, so many had been converted to God;

But amazingly, only the conversion of Saul of Tarsus

Had become so significant in the Christian life.

The main reason?

The mind-blowing paradigm shift happened in Saul's life.

It was not just changing his original name, Saul, into Paul,

As some of us may think of it

As sort of move from an immoral to a moral life.

Rather, it was "swing shift"

From a false notion of a holy life to a true one.

As Paul testified (Acts 22:3–16),

He had been a staunch believer, follower,

And ambitious leader

In his cradle religion where he was formed and groomed.

He was fuming with hatred against any new faith

That would be a threatening factor to his own.

But in one single moment of history,

An astronomical paradigm shift happened

In his mind-set:

Whatever he encountered, saw, and heard

Changed his "life move" topsy-turvy.

Becoming a Christian is not just a onetime event.

Nor is conversion something that happens once in a lifetime.

Indeed, most of us have undergone

Such multiple conversions

At different times, in different ways,

And for different purposes.

Let us ask ourselves now, as Paul testifies,

Have such conversions led us closer to the risen Jesus?

A deeper delving into His living waters?

If not, now is the right time. Thanks to God's mercy,

We are privileged to reach the golden age.

The good Lord has bestowed this golden opportunity

To make best use of it to encounter a genuine paradigm shift.

Let's be converted to Jesus, as Paul, totally

To enjoy the benefits of living and moving

In Christ's joy and peace, plus

To proclaim His good news to others until we meet the Lord.

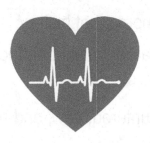

# 84. The Golden Age Is the Last but One Station Before God's Hilltop

During many decades of our past life,

We have been blessed with millions of hours of breathing.

As the Bible tells us, during those precious hours,

The Creator has designed events

And purposes of each moment

In accordance with the predestination of each one of us.

At each phase (I call it "station")

Of our life journey, lamentably,

We have wrongly used most of those hours

To be gratified fleshly

And to deviate from God's highway.

Thanks to God's mercy,

We too have rightly used many of them

To be forgiven and to rise and return to His highway.

As we have reached our golden age, the last but one station,

We are willy-nilly gifted with

More time to relax, more time to rest,

And gratefully more sufficient and more urgent time

To unroll the scroll of God's book to read His promises:

"I will make with them an eternal covenant,

Never to cease doing good to them;

Into their hearts I will put the fear of me,

That they may never depart from me" (Jer. 32:40).

Hear clearly the encouraging words

From Peter (1 Pet. 4:13–14):

"Rejoice beloved in the measure

That you share Christ's sufferings.

When his glory is revealed, you will rejoice exultantly."

Are we not really blessed for this precious golden age?

It is indeed an opportune time

As we are at the threshold of God's heavenly abode.

Come, let us make the best use of it

And get and enjoy all the divine gifts full to the brim.

# 85. Golden Results of the Sufferings at Golden Age

Looking back at my fifty years of ministry, I feel blessed

Not just by my caregiving services to the golden-agers

But much more by the lessons I learn from many of them

About how to live and feel great in my own golden age.

They have shown me what truly my humanity is;

They have showed me how I can be noble and great.

I have observed their tenacious daily efforts

To reach for higher things.

They are bedridden with pain and horrible uncured sickness.

Every day they see doctors and nurses posting the charts

On their ailment, getting worse with a predictable countdown.

Mind boggling, but in my visits,

I sense their poise and repose.

They remind me of Paul's mind-set (Phil. 3:13–14):

"I for my part do not consider myself

To have taken possession.

Just one thing: forgetting what lies behind

But straining forward to what lies ahead,

I continue my pursuit toward the goal,

The prize of God's upward calling, in Christ Jesus."

There is one particular moment

When my spirit has gotten greatly shook up.

Whenever I hold their hands warmly

And bend down to their ears, I lisp some scriptural words

In my usual preaching style:

"Please take all your sufferings

As the weapons of righteousness

And try to go through them with and for Christ so that

Your heavenly victory would be assured.

The yoke you bear would become easy and the burden light.

By doing this, you become a coredeemer as Mother Mary

Did in bringing abundant salvation to humanity."

The wonder of wonder is I have noticed

Their hands are gripping my hands tightly

Their heads nod with a big smile.

I honestly don't think I have done this.

These friends have already been shaped, groomed,

And filled with God's Spirit.

They only let me know such a marvelous thing is possible.

# 86. Let Us Watch out Our Cloudy Days

Most of the days in our ordinary life chores, our mood swings

From frustrated to questioning, from hopeful to devastated.

When we deal with God the Supreme,

The same back-and-forth swinging, in and out, hits—

From faithful to faithless, from religious to irreligious,

And from devotional to irreverential.

Many times, such reeling may turn

To be so rash and brash that

We may be pushed out of our balance.

Devastation will be the result.

This sort of bad roller coaster of life

Should be consciously dealt with,

Especially during the golden period of our life;

Otherwise, according to human vulnerability,

It will get worse to make us victimized

By too many unclean spirits of

Hardheadedness and blindfoldedness.

The venomous spirit of wounded pride

Will suck out our spiritual strength,

And finding no escape from them, our hearts,

Growing embittered, will mourn in utter pessimism,

*My life is nothing but a breath.*

*I have been roaming about as a mere phantom.*

*My life is a waste. All my accomplishments are in vain.*

*I am only a shadow and not a reality.*

*I am like an herb blooming in the morn*

*And being withered at the eventide.*

*Why should I fret over preserving my life?*

*Seventy years, eighty years, or one hundred and more?*

*What the heck! After all,*

*Most of them are toil and sorrow.*

*They pass quickly, and I am gone.*

*My life is set to end like a sigh.*

*It has started receding, being annihilated.*

While our hearts groan bitterly,

If they are not already disciplined and shaped,

They begin to bleed with acute anger

Against our past, our present, and our very self,

Blaming ourselves:

*I was stupid and did not understand, no better than a beast.*

*I had made my third eye wrecked and ruined.*

*I lost my ability to see anything truthful and salvific.*

My friends recovering from this devastation and frustration,

There is still some leftover time to claim a second chance.

Stop blaming yourselves and God.

Let us rise like the prodigal son from our blind sight.

Let us go to the same God who has brought us to this world

And who alone can extend

His merciful hands and uplift us.

Then we will see our golden age splendidly glittering.

# 87. An Amazing Age to Be Alive, Full to the Brim

Very often people around us spoil the Christian gladness
We have been endowed with at our baptism.
Now is the right time to claim it.
I uphold such enthralling belief only in the Lord's light
Whenever I come across
The scriptural passage (Luke 4:1–21)
Narrating Jesus's first appearance to the public.
Soon after His experiences both at baptism
And in the desert,
I hear the Lord say directly to me,
"The Spirit of the Lord is upon me,
Because he has anointed me
To bring glad tidings to the poor . . .
And to proclaim a year acceptable to the Lord."
He confirms to me He has been totally anointed
By God's Spirit.
I know this has happened throughout His life's journey,
From the moment of His conception in Mary's womb
Through the moments of His hidden life at Nazareth
And through the days of His public ministry.
At baptism, the Spirit has descended on Him like a dove;

After baptism, He has been led by the Spirit into the desert.

Then, He has begun His ministry in the power of the Spirit.

With this marvelous backdrop, He loudly announces to me,

"I bring glad tidings to you."

He details to me what His glad tidings are;

He will bring to me a better life of freedom

And a more genuine and wholistic healing.

As Gospel writers underwrite,

These glad tidings will be realized in me

If I repent and believe in Jesus and His teachings.

More applicably, He emphasizes He has come

To proclaim a year acceptable to the Lord.

That means, as I grasp, He points out to me

My golden age years are acceptable to the Lord.

Why and for what? I read His mind that

My golden age is the ripened time for reclaiming

My already inherited Christian gladness.

I am blessed by God to see and live to my golden age.

My Master's only desire is that

I should resolve to treat my golden age years

As Jubilee years of blessings of gladness

To me and to my relatives and friends.

I too will never forget

His two conditions for such reclaiming:

I should become poor in spirit and

Long and strive to be filled with His Spirit

More and more and more.

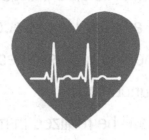

# 88. A Golden-Ager's Heart Gets More Golden By Being Inclusive

Of all that the church has taught me

In my early penny catechism classes,

Some have been agreeable to me,

Though a few of them are hard to dig into. For instance,

I find it easier to agree and accept that

God, in His wisdom and goodness, has

Created the universe with humans

According to His unfathomable purpose

Because, from my birth, I have been surrounded by

Large groups of humans believing

The same truth as absolute.

I also continue to believe but with some difficulty that

God has sent His Son, Jesus, to this world

To redeem His human creation

With His death and resurrection;

Plus, He has resolved to gather them together

As His chosen race and as His irreplaceable family,

And He has permitted Jesus's disciples

To name it "the church."

I have proudly but partly embraced the traditional lesson that

All the righteous, from Abel to the last of the elect,

Will be gathered in the church where, except the baptized,

All others are excluded.

Nonetheless, my mind might have reasonably agreed,

But my heart has found it hard to agreeably digest it.

However, I have been very happy

To learn one beautiful doctrine

Taught by the Vatican II on church in the modern world:

"All humans, despite their holdings

Different from my faith,

Are included in the Universal Church." It goes on listing that

They can be Jews, for whom the Son has been sent first;

Members of the Islamic faith, who worship one God;

Those who seek the unknown God

In darkness and shadows;

And even those who don't know Christ and His church

Yet seek God with a sincere heart and goodwill.

I have felt literally thrice blessed

As I have been lingering to get into Christian adulthood

To the extent of the full stature of Christ (Eph. 4:13–15).

Now being a golden-ager with a bit more godly wisdom,

The light of the modern church paves way

To attain my maturity.

Listening to and obeying Paul's admonition,

I have started attaining my Christian manhood

Not only by embracing the universal and inclusive

Nature of the church, the body of Christ,

But also by living every day of my life in love

And fully enjoying "unity in diversity."

As a remarkable effect of such holding,

I have begun realizing every one of my religious practices,

Getting new fervor and energy.

My heart has started beating the mantra

"This is the only way to grow in every way

Into Him, who is the head, Christ."

Wherever goodness, truth, and grace are found,

I begin seeking and finding the loved ones of God

Holding and hugging them with Gospel aroma

So that, on Judgment Day,

I will be rewarded as the Master's good and faithful servant.

# 89. The Untold Story of Many Daredevil Golden-Agers

A Tibetan proverb says, "It is better to live one day as a tiger

Than a thousand days as a sheep."

This is the sparkling viewpoint that urges

Some among us to become daredevils in their life.

These chivalrous men and women define "life"

As an adventure, challenge, enterprise, and so on.

They choose a unique traveling pattern

And march onto new horizons

Whenever and wherever life takes them to.

Their only preoccupation is to accomplish

Something great out of nothing great.

Some of their backgrounds are so ordinary that

They even do not recollect where

And how they have been born.

Everything around them is very ordinary, simple,

Sometimes absurd as most of us feel.

However, they pick up the pieces,

Get up and walk, run, surf, climb, swim, dive, ski,

And struggle to the last round. They never stop.

They are never satisfied with what they achieve temporarily.

All the interim achievements and failures are only

The stepping stones to go further, forward, and beyond.

Smart golden-agers too, in the light of Christ,

Take life as a journey of faith swamped with challenges.

They have learned by life's boxing that

Earthly life is simply a travel package

Full of numerous departures and arrivals.

Consciously, they ascertain that their life of long years,

Starting from ordinary beginnings,

Proceeding through uphills and downhills,

Will be ended with an extraordinary reach of eternity.

They are convinced that they are not citizens of this world

But sojourners and pilgrims in the voyage to the Beyond,

Whom they reverently call God, living in eternity—

In timeless time, spaceless space, and limitless limit.

Having been granted a gift of wisdom,

They already perceive that their voyage to eternity

Is not that easy and cozy. They have already encountered

An evil force staying within them and around them,

Prowling around like a roaring lion,

Looking for someone to devour.

It enforces them by his subliminal allurements

To be fully fastened to the temporary resorts and trivialities,

To weasel out of the life-winning responsibilities,

To be discouraged by unexpected life's turnings,

To be self-centered, and even to hurt other people's life.

They know all these, especially in their golden age.

The flabbergasting story is, among golden-agers, I discover

There are numerous friends leading a daredevil life

In combating the evil force.

Abiding by the exhortation of Peter (1 Pet. 5:8–10),

They have learned to be sober and vigilant, steadfast in faith.

Every day they reread with unremitting hope

The encouraging words of Peter:

"The God of all grace who called you

To his eternal glory through Christ Jesus will himself

Restore, confirm, strengthen, and establish you

After you have suffered a little."

# SECTION IV

# ABOUT GOLDEN AGE FINALE

# 90. The Results of Golden-Agers' Life

Under the heavy influence of the Almighty,

The good-willed soul of every golden-ager

Pines and longs for a quality life.

It is a life of contentment,

A life of fullness of peace,

A life of complete joy,

A life of mature love,

A life of absolutism.

And over and above all,

A golden-ager's soul aches for a seemingly fairy-tale life

Of eternity consisting of all the above listed.

Many golden-agers who are attuned to

Holy Scriptures and church tradition

Yearn and hanker for a Christ-centered life

To be possessed already in this world, in which

They have heavenly bread as their food;

They taste and relish, at least partially, life to its fullness;

They drink, bathe, and swim in the living waters;

They dwell every moment of their life

In the house of the Lord;

They climb up every step in the bright hope
Of reaching the hilltop;
They are holy as their heavenly Father is;
They live a resurrected life, moving with Jesus, alive.
Indeed, that is the story of every saint, like St. Athanasius:
"I ache to become god
As the Word became Man."

# 91. The Magnificent Last Wish of Golden-Agers

Most of our friends enjoying their golden age,

Unfortunately, are fretting over too much about

How their burial should be conducted and so on.

There is nothing wrong about it. But it shouldn't be

A source of disturbance in our final season.

Our preoccupation must be all focused on

How to stand before our Judge with our head held high.

We read in St. Augustine's *Confessions*

About an incident occurring at the final days of his mother.

While her sons have been very much worried about

Their farewell to be given to their mother

And discussing her burial to be done

Not far from home but in her own country, she tells them,

"What silly talk!

Lay this body anywhere, and take no trouble over it.

One thing only do I ask of you, that you remember me

At the altar of the Lord wherever you may be."

Saying such faith-filled words, she has fallen silent.

As a role model of how a Christian should conduct oneself

In the final stage of life's travel, Monica was feeling

So happy that The Lord had answered her lifelong prayer

For her son Augustine's conversion.

In that spirit of fulfillment, her heart was beating

Only thankful music to God.

She was fully prepared to go to Him.

Nothing had mattered to her.

This is the way all golden-agers must fly away—smilingly

To their Creator and the Redeemer.

# 92. Freeing from Fear of Death

For God, death is not an option.

His one and only option is life—

Life that is built on justice,

Life that is permeating with truth and nothing but truth,

Life that is sweating and bleeding in love sharing,

Life that is filled with hope, joy, and peace.

Death is not human life's climax, nor is it an end.

It is only a change of mode in life.

Its climax is to be fully with God.

Every living organism is said

To be changing itself every seven years.

Like it or not,

We undergo many deaths physically and mentally.

When our umbilical card is cut from our mother,

Our tender, cozy life meets, in a way, tiny death.

When we become youth, our childhood dies.

When we reach adulthood, our teen life disappears.

When we attain the golden age,

The vibrant adult life evaporates.

So when we breathe our last, our final death occurs,

A little bigger than other changes

But more profitable than they have been.

While other deaths have brought

Temporary goody-goody resorts,

The final death contributes to us the resort of eternity.

# 93. What Shall We Encounter in Our Finale?

If we believe there exists an inner spirit within our body,

We too accept an inner eye exists;

We can label it as third eye.

We agree fully with Paul about our third eye's low ability

To see through spiritual things:

"At present we see indistinctly, as in a mirror . . .

At present I know partially" (1 Cor. 13:12).

But after closing indefinitely our two physical eyes,

Our third eye will widely open.

As Paul utters, we will see face-to-face. What is it?

Since the inexpressible ray of light

Has already been sent in us

By the Word and His blood and by His sacraments,

We will see clearly two ineffable things:

One, the Almighty in His fullness. With John, we believe

"We are God's children now;

What we shall be has not yet been revealed.

We do know that . . .

We shall see him as he is" (1 John 3:2).

Two, the bittersweet biographical story of earthly life.

As its first part, we will spiritually discover our past life

That has been twisted, messed up, wasted away in vain.

It has been confirmed by the Lord's words:

"There is nothing concealed that will not be revealed

Nor secret that will not be known" (Luke 12:2–3).

As its second part, we will see through heavenly lenses

The stunning salvific deeds of the Triune God,

Which happened on my crisscross roadways of earthly life

With all their bloody but flowery backdrops as reality show.

What else can I say to you, my friends?

I can only repeat the golden words of St. Augustine:

"I implore you to live with me and,

By believing, to run with me;

Let us long for our heavenly country,

Let us sigh for our heavenly home,

Let us truly feel that here we are strangers."

# 94. God's Shema to Golden-Agers at Their Finale

I am so impressed and so joyful

Whenever I come across the holy words of God in scriptures,

Especially words about His "just ones" at the brink of their life.

Our God wants us to listen to them often,

Mainly when we are slowly losing

The physical grip of our senses.

I fondly title them as "Shema (listen) words"

And treasure them not in my pocket but in my chest:

"Blessed are the dead who die in the Lord from now on."

'Yes,' said the Spirit, 'let them find rest from their labors,

For their works accompany them." (Rev. 14:13).

"Well done, my good and faithful servant.

Since you were faithful in small matters,

I will give you great responsibilities.

Come, share your master's joy" (Matt. 25:23).

"Come, you who are blessed by my Father.

Inherit the kingdom prepared for you

From the foundation of the world" (Matt. 25:34).

"Amen, I say to you,

Today you will be with me in Paradise" (Luke 23:43).

The Lord exhorts us to *listen* to
All the above-mentioned biblical words,
Which will be the light to our path to finale
And will be our food and drink as viaticum
As we will be heading to eternal life.

# 95. Can Our Dream about Our Own Death Come True?

I am sure most of us are acquainted with

One popular baby boomer Christopher Eric Hitchens

With his life and controversial ideologies.

Once, he portrayed his dream of dying in *Hitch-22*:

"I personally want to 'do' death

In the active and not the passive,

And to be there to look it in the eye

And be doing something when it comes for me."

At the age of sixty-two, he died of pneumonia,

A complication of esophageal cancer.

Before he died, he was quoted in *Vanity Fair* saying,

"In whatever kind of a 'race' life may be,

I have very abruptly become a finalist."

There were in history many such dreamers of death,

Starting from Jesus to millions of His followers.

Indeed, Jesus, being very close to the divine,

Predicted about His ignominious death and its follow-up.

But He never forgot to underline that

"It is all in My Father's hands."

He also exhorted His followers not to be anxious

About death; He preferred to call it positively as

*The arrival of the Son of Man.*

He also affirmed its time and place, known only by His Father;

Plus, about the aftermath of our death—

Blessed and cursed—

He avowed it solely depended on the Father.

The funny thing about me is,

Once, I have read in a social media article

That we will die in the same position

As we are used to in sleep.

Hence, one day I have kept near my bed

My camera rolling the whole night.

I have woken up and begun browsing the film shot.

I have just giggled to myself because I have never seen

Any dead body in the casket in that way.

Then and there, I have resolved, "What the heck,

In life and death, I am in His hands."

That suffices to me.

# 96. At the End of the Day

Jesus has tried to portray our relationship with Him

By beautiful different metaphors.

One among them is that of a master and his servants.

In the same vein, He has also offered a metaphor

To explain His relationship with His stewards.

His stewards are those to whom

He delegates His job of leading His people and

Managing His kingdom until He comes again.

He wants them

Not to be unjust stewards (Luke 16:1–13) but

To be faithful and farsighted stewards (Matt. 24:45–51).

He will either reward or punish His stewards

According to their industrious use of the gifts

He has entrusted to them (Matt. 25:14–30);

Plus, He forewarns them about

The tragedy of being stripped off

Their power, prestige, and rights on His arrival

If they destroy the holiness of His kingdom

By their abusive, wicked deeds (Matt. 21:33–41).

Those stewards who waste their lifetime

In debasing themselves will be severely punished

At the end of their earthly days

By their Master, who is justice and truth.

If they have performed their duties well

In making God's kingdom grow,

The same Master, who is goodness and greatness,

Will reward them lavishly

With unending peace, joy, and glory.

Every moment God's Spirit invites the golden-agers

Who have been delegated by Him

To lead many people for many years

In His kingdom in one way or another

And to whom He has granted

Some more precious time of breathing in the golden age

To make the best use of the balanced time

In revisiting their past

And to beg the Master's mercy to rewrite

Their debauched stewardship

So that, at the end of the day,

They may hear a kindly voice within them, saying,

"Well done, My faithful, forgiven steward.

Come and enjoy your reward as I have promised."

# 97. To Golden-Agers, Death Is a Friend

I have been astounded to hear many golden-agers
Saying to me,
"Death is not as I was once thinking.
It is not an enemy to me.
It is not a last stop of my life either.
Rather, it is a threshold of the 'lasting life.'"
Their assessment is absolutely correct.
Death is a final line for takeoff in our human soul's flight
(Maybe with a bit of noise, tremor, gasping, and so on)
Toward rejoining the Synergy, whom we call God,
To and for whom our energy, with all its essence and frame,
Is indebted and aching.
Death is not altogether a full stop but a comma or
Semicolon in our love letter to our beloved, the Supreme.
It is because of this enlightened view that
Death has lost its terror over my beloved golden-agers;
Rather, it has turned out to be a friendly medium
For realizing two of their life's purposes:
One, it makes easy their action plan to realize
One of their topmost dreams in life.
I am a dreamer of too many dreams

About my prosperity and development.

I know well it is very easy to dream but hard as hell

To execute the plan and to realize my ambitious dreams.

The biggest dream in life of any good-willed human is

To live forever, never dying, and to be eternal.

And it is true with my elderly friends.

They are ready to meet death because they perceive it well

As a jump start to get into their long-awaited eternity.

Through a single stroke, a tiny strike,

Death comes in; humans are out there in a flash

To a sphere of timeless time and spaceless space.

They also recognize that by death, they will be liberated

From all their pains, worries, and burdens of sicknesses.

Two, my senior friends uphold with scriptural insight

That human death, by the powerful action of Jesus,

Has become their purifying medium,

A bloody but straight path to sanctity, a blessing in disguise.

They completely agree with St. Paul:

"If we have been united with him in a death like his,

We will certainly be united with him

In a resurrection like his" (Rom. 6:5).

Praised be to the Lord!

With my friendly golden-agers, I thank God

For such a great gift of death bestowed to us,

With which our lifeline is clear and straight.

I am also struck with wonder after noticing

How my neighborly golden-agers are

Preparing themselves for meeting death

In a friendly and productive way:

To die with Jesus and be buried with Jesus.

It is not merely to make arrangements

To receive the anointing of the sick,

Not just working with a funeral home

For a Christian burial and so on.

More than anything else,

While they are still alive, they make it a daily habit

To exercise and practice the act of dying,

Namely, dying to selfishness and dying to sin.

Then they assure themselves that

Death will be a dear friend to them

As it has been to Jesus, paving the way for His resurrection.

# 98. Our Death Is Precious but Very Costly

It is hard to observe people dying;

Even thinking of it troubles us

And brings nightmares in sleep.

Worst of all, we become downhearted

As we are incapacitated by old age, though it is golden,

And when we are told by our physician

That our death is not far.

God never nullifies it but encourages us to face it positively.

He asserts through His Son that

"He is not God of the dead, but of the living" (Luke 20:38).

Those words echo what God has said earlier (Ws 1:13):

"God did not make death,

Nor does he rejoice in the destruction of the living."

The real reason for death is the devil (Ws 2:23–24):

"For God formed us to be imperishable;

The image of his own nature he made us.

But by the envy of the devil, death entered the world,

And they who are allied with him experience it."

Is this biblical statement sufficient for us

To accept death smilingly?

God knows we won't be satisfied with it

Because He knows that we know

Death is inevitable for any physical living creature.

Still, He firmly acknowledges

Through the psalmist (116:15)

"O precious in the eyes of the Lord is the death of his faithful,"

Meaning there is a vast difference between

The death of the faithful and that of the wicked:

"The souls of the righteous are in the hand of God,

And no torment shall touch them.

They seemed, in the view of the foolish, to be dead;

And their passing away was thought an affliction

And their going forth from us, utter destruction.

But they are in peace" (Ws 3:1–3).

This is possible for the faithful because, as Paul ascertains,

"If we live, we live for the Lord,

And if we die, we die for the Lord;

So then, whether we live or die,

We are the Lord's" (Rom. 14:8).

# 99. The Way Golden-Agers
# Meet Death in Its Den

In the age of wisdom, I mean at the nightfall of old age,

So many of us are overanxious about how to pull through

Our golden years of earthly life.

Some say, "Death is my greatest fear."

Many others say, "I feel I should not dwell too much

On my final hours. This is because,

By such freaking out, I may lose my grip

Over the present day,

And it might debilitate my valor to avail the residue of life."

To be freed of death anxiety, some others frankly confess,

"I distribute some of my possessions and savings

To my loved ones, some to philanthropic

And religious causes.

And with the rest of my savings,

I travel around the world, visit casinos,

Play golf, go skydiving,

And surely enjoy myself with right but new food and drinks."

After reading the above and more assertions,

I think of my own views about my death.

In my muddle age, I have had the feeling of fear about death.

I am now mature to accept

Yes, I will die.

Yes, I don't want to know the day and time of it

Because I want to act like its villain

To meet it face-to-face.

Yes, I didn't save a lot of money

In bonds, stocks, or properties.

But as the money comes, I have already given some of them

To charities, to the needy;

Plus, I have written in my will

If anything is left as my savings, it must go to good causes.

Yes, my spending is frugal

Except for my health maintenance.

Yes, my food and others have been rationed by my diabetes.

There's one more thing I do

While waiting to fight against death:

I make sure I uphold my faithfulness to my God, and

I have exercised my heart to beat,

*Lord Jesus Christ,*

*Son of the Living God,*

*Have mercy on me, a sinner.*

Faithfully and honestly, I live on every day

As a living sacrifice of praise to God.

# 100. Golden-Agers' Death Is Not a Failure but a Victory

Our death is very costly, as we have talked about earlier,

Not in the sense of dollars for the funeral charges;

Rather, it demands from us to make it a sacrificial offering.

We too have said our death is precious in the eyes of God

Not because God is a sadist

To enjoy seeing our gasping for breath

But because it is the only way to covet our ultimate reward.

Jesus has clearly announced the good and great News that

"Then the righteous will shine like the sun

In the kingdom of their Father" (Matt. 13:43).

Death is a rightful and authentic answer

To the continuous prayer of golden-agers as David has done:

"One thing I ask of the Lord; this I seek:

To dwell in the Lord's house all the days of my life,

To gaze on the Lord's beauty, to visit his temple" (Ps. 27:4).

As St. Ambrose writes, God demonstrates

The efficacy and valuableness of human death

Through His beloved Son Jesus's death.

Exorbitantly and in a mind-boggling way,

God has bestowed the grace of salvation to humanity

Only by the ignominious death of Jesus.

His death has amazingly become a source of life for all of us.

As Jesus has won the victory against evil,

Our death, connected with Christ, will become

The way to attain victory over our evils;

And in line with it,

We will be crowned with heavenly resurrection.

Therefore, we can boldly live and declare, like Paul,

"Now as always, Christ will be magnified in my body,

Whether by life or by death.

For to me life is Christ, and death is gain" (Phil. 1:20–21).

In the meantime, let us exercise ourselves

As a steadfast preparation to meet "our final death"

By undergoing small deaths in everyday life.

Here is how I exercise daily for a victorious death.

Every morning as I get up from my bed, I sing,

*"Ready to go, ready to go to the house the Lord.*

*Ready to climb, ready to climb up the mountain of the Lord.*

*I have been baptized in Jesus.*

*By His blood, I have been cleansed.*

*He is my Good Shepherd.*

*I am His baby sheep,*

*Lost but found by Him."*

# OTHER BOOKS BY THE AUTHOR

SONDAY SONRISE: Homilies for Sundays and
 Solemnities of Years ABC
DAILY DOSE FOR CHRISTIAN SURVIVAL:
Daily Scriptural Meditation and Spiritual Medication
PRAYERFULLY YOURS: Qualityprayer for Qualitylife
CATHOLIC CHRISTIAN SPIRITUALITY for New Age
 Dummies
MY RELIGION: REEL OR REAL?
A Postmodern Catholic's Assessment of His Religion
MINISTRY IN TEARS: International Priests' Missionary
 Life and Ministry
(coauthored by Rev. Dasan Vima, SJ)
HILLTOP MEDITATIONS Vol. I:
Reflections on Scriptural Readings of Sundays and
 Festivals of Years A&B
HILLTOP MEDITATIONS Vol. II:
Reflections on Scriptural Readings of Sundays and
 Festivals—Year C
BLESSED THE MERCIFUL:
Description of Chesed-Oriented Christian Life
LIVING FAITH DAILY in spirit and in truth
DISCIPLED LEADERSHIP:
The Nuts and Bolts of Being Successful Parish Leaders